Your Future & You

Your Future & You

Marriage . . . Priesthood,
Religious Life, Single Life?

James Finley

Ave Maria Press • Notre Dame, Ind. 46556

First printing, March, 1981
Second printing, August, 1984
58,000 copies in print

Permissions and credits:

Excerpts from the English translation of the *Rite of Marriage* 1969, International Committee on English in the Liturgy, Inc. All rights reserved.

Excerpts from: Thomas Merton, *The Wisdom of the Desert.* © 1960 by The Abbey of Gethsemani, Inc. Reprinted by permission of New Directions.

Unless otherwise noted, scripture texts used in this work are taken from the *New American Bible,* copyright © 1970 by the Confraternity of Christian Doctrine, Washington, D.C., and are used by permission of the copyright owner. All rights reserved.

All quotes of Vatican II documents are taken from *The Documents of Vatican II,* Walter M. Abbott, S.J. (New York: America Press, 1966).

© 1981 by Ave Maria Press, Notre Dame, Indiana 46556
All rights reserved.

Library of Congress Catalog Card Number: 81-65228
International Standard Book Number: 0-87793-223-9

Photography:
    Terry Barrett, 46; Eugene S. Geissler, 68; Jack Hamilton, 144; Howard Johnson, 91; Kellner's Photo Services, 26; William Koechling, 132; Freda Leinwand, 38, 101, 158; Jean-Claude Lejeune, 85, 95, 110; Tom McGuire, cover, 75, 150; Carolyn A. McKeone, 80; Frank Methe, 53; Patrick Mooney, 50, 126, 138; Notre Dame Printing and Publications Office, 118, 162; Religious News Service, cover; Steven Rogers, 166; Jeri Schwartz, 172; Rick Smolan, 21; Bob Taylor, cover; Jim Witmer, cover, 8.

Manufactured in the United States of America.

To my wife
Kaye Robbins Finley
and our children
Kelly and Amy

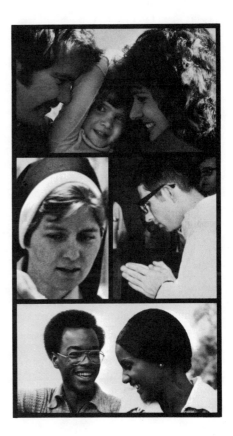

Acknowledgments

I wish to thank the following people whose support and combined efforts have made it possible for me to write this book.

My wife Kaye is deserving of a special word of thanks. Much of what is written here about marriage can be attributed to her love, encouragement and insightful suggestions. Father Bill Schooler and Marianne Doran worked closely with me from the very beginning of this project. Father Bill's numerous editorial improvements and Marianne's typing of both the pilot and final draft of the manuscript are greatly appreciated. Frank Cunningham and the rest of the Ave Maria staff have, as usual, given me their competent and kind assistance. Bishop William McManus of the Fort Wayne-South Bend Diocese encouraged me in the planning stages of the pilot by his personal interest in the book as well as by his commitment to religious education in general. My friend, Michael Pennock, made a number of helpful suggestions in his critique of the pilot. Cy DeVleigher, the other administrators, and my fellow teachers at Marian High School have been cooperative and patient with the inconveniences caused by my writing and lecturing commitments. Finally, I extend an expression of gratitude to my students at Marian High School. I hope that the sense of challenge and pleasure I feel in being their religion teacher have been apparent in the pages of this book.

The following people have read and responded to the first drafts of the manuscript or have offered some other form of assistance: Bob and Pat Schultheis, Leonard and Bernie Micinski, Mark and Rita Muzzilo, Mary Frances Kazinski, Mike Piechnik, Jeff Iacobazzi, Anita Zepeda, Barb Bauters, Joan Holland, Father Charles Conley and Sister Joyce Diltz.

James Finley

Contents

1 We Have Been Friends Together 9

2 Romantic-Sexual Love 27

3 Marriage in Scripture 47

4 Marriage in the Tradition of the Church 69

5 Some Practical Concerns of Married Couples 95

6 The Priesthood and the Religious Life 119

7 The Single Life 159

  Epilogue 169

1

We Have Been Friends Together

Seek eagerly after love.
—St. Paul

Few questions are of greater importance in adult life than those involving marriage. This book is written to help you face these questions with a greater degree of understanding of some of the basic elements of married life. While looking at marriage from a number of different perspectives, our primary vantage point will be that of faith. In other words, we will be examining *Christian marriage* as a vocation, as a way of following Christ by means of a growing union with one's spouse and children.

Although our reflections will be primarily about marriage, we will also examine the single life as well as the priesthood and religious life. In short, this book is about your future. It is written to help you face those decisions which will have deep and far-reaching effects upon your life and the lives of those around you.

In turning first to marriage, we will attempt to answer two fundamental questions: *What is the nature of that love which binds a man and woman together as one flesh until death? And What can young men and women do to prepare themselves for this love?*

9

Your Idea of Marriage

As a way of getting started, do the following exercise. It is intended to help you become aware of some attitudes you and your classmates have toward marriage.

Gather into small groups of all boys or all girls. The boys' groups are asked to make a list of what they consider to be the 10 most important qualities of the ideal wife. The girls' groups are asked to make a similar list describing the ideal husband. After the lists are completed, each group should put its list in order by arranging the items in the list from the most to the least important. Compare and discuss the lists as a class.

Ask your parents to make a similar list at home. Bring the parents' lists to class to be discussed and compared with the students' lists.

Marriage as Friendship

Raissa Maritain, wife of the famous philosopher Jacques Maritain, wrote a book describing the way she and Jacques met, fell in love and married. The title of her book, *We Have Been Friends Together,* aptly describes the theme of this first chapter of our study of marriage; namely, *marriage is a unique form of friendship.*

Ideally speaking, a husband and wife should be each other's best friend. Of course, a husband and wife are not simply friends. They are also lovers. Romantic-sexual love gives the friendship of marriage its unique character. We will discuss romantic-sexual love at length in Chapter Two, along with the love that comes with being parents. But in this chapter we will be concerned with one fundamental fact about married love: a happy, lifelong marriage is a happy, lifelong friendship.

Marriage is unique. There is no other relationship that involves a lifelong commitment to such intimacy and sharing. It is the love of friendship warmed by romance that allows this intimacy and sharing to mature, deepen and endure. Such intimacy and sharing are all but impossible between two people who are not the best of friends or who feel indifferent or distant from each other.

Since marriage requires friendship, understanding some of the basic dynamics of friendship can provide insights into married life. In other words, a young person preparing for eventual marriage should examine his or her present stage of development in the art of friendship.

Sit quietly for a moment. Think of your best friends. Then write five statements about friendship, each beginning with the words,

"A friend is . . ."

After everyone is finished, put the best two or three statements from each list on the board and discuss. Finally, replace the phrase, "A friend," with the phrase, "A husband or wife." What does this suggest about the relationship between friendship and marriage?

The Love of Self

Self-love may seem like a strange way to begin reflecting on friendship and marriage. Very often the term self-love is used to imply the notion of being selfish, that is, of tending to love one's self instead of or at the price of others. But here we are using the term self-love in the positive and constructive sense of *recognizing our own worth and dignity as a person capable of loving and being loved.* Self-love gives us the confidence needed to reveal and give ourselves in friendship. Likewise, the lack of self-love threatens friendship. For when self-love is lacking, we isolate ourselves from others in the fear they will discover the unlovable person we imagine ourselves to be. Thus, growth in self-love is vital to friendship and hence, to marriage.

Growing in Self-Love through Reaching for Goals

One way in which we grow in self-love is by learning to recognize and put into practice our own unique gifts and talents. This process of self-discovery is not without its painful moments. A part-time job, a challenging course in school, going out for a sport or learning to play a musical instrument may reveal to us what we *cannot* do as well as what we can do. But the most important things are those we learn about ourselves in the process of attempting to reach our goals.

A small child takes many falls in the process of learning how to walk. And in doing so, he or she learns much more than simply the skill of walking. The child begins to recognize something of his or her own worth as a person who is willing to take risks in order to grow and learn about life.

Similarly, whether or not you succeed in getting an "A" on a chemistry exam or making the first string of the basketball team or getting the lead role in a school play is, in the long run, secondary to the *qualities* you develop within yourself as you try to meet your goals.

Helen Keller is a striking and classic example of this. Her story continues to inspire millions of children and adults, not primarily because she learned to communicate with others in spite of her severe physical handicaps, but because of her tremendous courage in struggling to overcome her handicaps. Her dignity as a person shines through her refusal to be overcome by obstacles that make our own problems seem small by comparison. More than learning how to communicate, she learned the art of living life to the full.

---

1. Who are some other famous people who had to struggle against severe handicaps or other obstacles? Do these heroes and heroines all seem to possess the self-love we are discussing here, that is, do they each appear to be aware of their dignity and worth as a person?

2. Indicate two or three qualities or strengths that might emerge in a high school student as he or she works toward achieving each of the following goals:

- helping elderly people in the neighborhood

- struggling against some personal fault or weakness such as a bad temper

- being active in school sports *an achiever physical strength*
- maintaining a part-time job *servileness politeness*

After all are finished, share your answers by indicating how each quality mentioned might help a person be a good friend. How would each quality be important in marriage? *Each help the pair to get along better + be more aware of the others personhood*

3. People who feel insecure about their own worth often tend to be either overly aggressive or very withdrawn from others. Discuss why these effects of a lack of self-love would tend to have serious negative effects in school, in dating and in other social involvements. Why would they make marriage difficult? What might the following marriages be like: a) between two aggressive people; b) between two withdrawn people; c) between an aggressive and a withdrawn person?

they would prevent because they getting you along w/ others don't listen or respect each others thoughts

To much to themselves — can't share w/ each other

One is too strong & the other too weak

4. Discuss the statement: You cannot love another unless you also love yourself. *You can't feel respect for anyone else unless you respect yourself.*

to this

Growing in Self-Love through Loving Others

Even more than striving toward goals, friends help us to develop self-love. True friendship is not based on achievements, possessions or talents. A friend is not a friend because of anything he or she owns or has achieved, but simply because of *who* he or she is. Friendship is based upon a mutual love that allows two people to recognize in each other their unique, mysterious value as persons.

In loving our friends, we help them realize they are worth all that love offers. And our friends' love for us reveals to us our worth as a person. Thus, it is in loving and being loved that friends offer to one another the gift of discovering the dignity of being a person.

This does not mean that friendship is a free ride to mutual, unencumbered love of self and others. Sometimes our friends let us down. And sometimes we fail to love our friends as we should. But even when such human mistakes take place, there is a potential for both friends to help one another grow in genuine self-love, as long as both continue to have faith in one another and the love they share. Like two children learning to walk together, friends can help one another to their feet again, and encourage each other to continue growing.

Seen in this way, every friendship prepares the way for the unique friendship of marriage. Every friendship helps us grow in that self-love that allows us to open and give ourselves to others.

---

1. Go back to the exercise in which you completed the phrase, "A friend is. . . ." Rewrite some of your responses on the board. Then erase the opening phrase, "A friend is," and replace it with, "I am. . . ." What does this suggest about the role of friendship in helping us discover our worth as a person?

2. List on the board and discuss some of the specific ways that husbands and wives can and should help one another to discover and grow in the awareness of their dignity as persons, for example, by expressing appreciation for some small act of kindness.

GIVE 3 EXAMPLES

The Love of Others

Self-love makes friendship possible. But two people do not become friends simply because they have each developed a high degree of awareness of their own dignity as persons. Friendship begins only when two people start to love and care about each other.

Love that is not given away turns sour. Self-love that is not used as a means of loving others tends to deteriorate into selfishness. The destructive nature of selfishness is graphically portrayed in the Greek myth of the young man Narcissus, who fell in love with his own image reflected on the surface of a lake. His love for himself became so strong that he was aware of nothing else. He was eventually turned into a narcissus, a flower which the Greeks considered to be a symbol of death.

There is a Narcissus in each of us. That is, within each of us there is a tendency to turn in upon ourself to the exclusion of everyone else. In infancy, this tendency is normal. An infant is not capable of returning and sharing the love it receives from its parents. But as a child matures, he or she learns to love and care about others.

This learning to share and give love continues throughout our lives. Our friends are especially important in this growth process. Learning to be a friend means learning to share, care, give and be open with another. Seen in this way, every friendship plays its part in preparing a young person for marriage, a relationship in which two people share and give their very lives in love to one another and to their children.

Going Out of Your Way

The expression "going out of your way to help another" is helpful in understanding a basic aspect of loving others. "Your way" implies all that leads to your own pleasure and fulfillment.

We do not mind doing things for ourselves, because we know that all our efforts will "pay off" in the end by helping us reach some desired object or goal. A young man or woman, for example, might work after school at some unpleasant job in order to get enough money to buy a car or a stereo. Others might study long hours in order to be accepted by a prestigious college. All of these things are fine. In fact, they serve to demonstrate the discipline needed to develop our skills and talents in the fostering of genuine self-love.

But the test of true friendship begins in the effort needed to go out of our way to help and give ourselves to another. This mutual sensitivity and concern for another is essential to any mature and lasting friendship as well as to the unique friendship of marriage.

The quality of a marriage depends precisely on the extent to which both partners have learned to go beyond themselves in loving concern for the needs of the other. It takes two pulling together, each centered in the other, to bring about the happiness and fulfillment love offers. Paradoxically, this willingness to forego our own selfish needs in love for another brings a fullness into our life which is beyond description. It is, in other words, in *giving* ourselves in love that we *receive* the happiness love brings.

Listed below are a number of occasions in which you might be asked to "go out of your way" to help another. Under each item indicate the degree to which you yourself find this situation difficult to do (letting 1 equal the least, and 5, the most degree of difficulty). Then, under each line, suggest what each activity can do to enrich your life or what it can teach you about growing in love for others.

Visiting or writing to a grandparent.

1 2 3 4 5

Helping a younger brother or sister with schoolwork.

1 2 3 4 5

Intentionally not going out on a date in order to spend a night with the family or talking to your parents.

1 2 3 4 5

Doing extra work around the house without being asked when you see your parents are especially bogged down.

1 2 3 4 5

Taking the trouble to talk to a student at school who appears to have few or no friends.

1 2 3 4 5

Married life offers numerous occasions for a husband and wife to go out of their way for one another. When they do so they discover that their two ways merge and become one in their loving sensitivity to each other's needs.

In marriage, a husband and wife are called to a sensitivity and mutual self-giving that is both rewarding and challenging. A husband and wife live in an intimacy that invites a sensitive response to one another's most fundamental physical, emotional and spiritual needs.

An example of this is that of a wife who feels depressed because her husband and older children seem to give no indication they appreciate all she does as she cares for their needs. When her husband comes home from work, she expresses her need for love and recognition by acting irritable and upset.

How he responds to her signals of distress is important to her. He will make matters worse if he ignores her unspoken plea for appreciation by walking in the door, asking when supper will be ready and then burying his face in the newspaper. His wife needs him to be sensitive and caring enough to sit down, talk and find out what is bothering her. When he realizes the problem, he could assure her that in the future he will try harder to lighten her burden and to express his gratitude for all she does for him. If there are children old enough to understand, he might talk to them, encourage them to be more aware of what their mother does and how they can avoid making her work unnecessarily difficult.

This sensitivity and going out of one's way must be *mutual*. Both husband and wife must do their sincere best to remain open to and aware of each other's needs. Such sensitivity must be accompanied by a great deal of patience. Very often both spouses will fail to be the perfect, sensitive partner. For example, in our story the husband may fail to respond to his wife's needs because he is discouraged over some problem or excited over some good news that came up at work.

Most importantly, this going out of one's way is the very work of love that holds a marriage together and allows it to grow. The work of love consists of the lifetime effort of learning how to care, listen, be open and concerned about another.

Below is a list of fundamental needs. Gather into small groups, and using the above story as a model, think of similar situations that describe how these needs are met or not met.

To accomplish this, do the following:

a) Make up a specific scene or incident in married life in which this need might be expressed.

b) Suggest an attitude or way of acting that would indicate the spouse is being insensitive to the need being expressed.

c) Finally, suggest an attitude or way of acting that would indicate a sensitivity and willingness to go out of one's way to respond to the need being expressed.

Reflect upon the fundamental need to be. . .

- appreciated and respected as a person........

- heard and understood....

- forgiven...........................

- helped in making a serious decision ....

- able to express and share love for God........

- held, shown affection......

- share happiness..............

- be consoled in a time of worry or anxiety............

Christian Faith and Married Love

Our Christian faith is extremely helpful in learning to love one's self and others. Christian faith enhances friendship and gives new meaning to married love.

The faith dimension of genuine self-love is revealed in the Book of Genesis: "God created man in his image; in the Divine image he created him" (Gn 1:27). When personally accepted as God's living word, this text has profound implications concerning our growth in self-love. For in the passage, God tells us that we are like him. In our inmost center we are essentially good, because we are like God who is goodness itself. We may have reason to doubt the goodness of something we have done. But we cannot doubt the goodness of who we are, without in some way doubting God, in whose image we are made.

Our faith clearly acknowledges the reality of sin and our unworthiness before God. In the book of Genesis God reveals to us that our sense of guilt and confusion in our failures to reach unity with ourselves and others results from our loss of unity with God through sin (Gn 3). But even here God reveals to us the faith dimension of self-love. For in their sin Adam and Eve receive God's promise to send One who will crush the forces of evil (Gn 3:15).

The *Covenant* given to Moses is a sign of God's love for us. In the light of the Covenant every Jew was able to see himself or herself as tenderly loved and cared for by God who "remembers not our sin." In the Covenant God reveals that our sins will never cast a shadow over his absolute and faithful love for his children. The message of the Old Testament seems clear: How can we doubt ourselves when God loves us so? Or, as Saint Paul writes in the New Testament, "If God is on our side then who can be against us?" (Rom 9:31).

The Old Testament also gives us the faith dimension for loving others. The love God has for us, he has for all his children. We must, therefore, love others in recognition of our common bond in the love of God. The Ten Commandments express this clearly. The first three commandments stress the need to "love God above all things." The last seven commandments stress that we must "love our neighbor as ourselves" in order to love God above all things. That is, we must love ourselves and others in order to be united with God who loves us all as his children.

The Book of Jonah is very short. Read it to yourself quietly. Then as a class, discuss its message about the need to love others as God loves us.

In turning to the New Testament we note first that Christ is God's supreme revelation of our worth and dignity in his eyes. Out of love for us, God took upon himself our humanity. He lived our life and died our death that we might have eternal life. No one can take the Gospel seriously without seeing in Christ a revelation of his or her own self-worth.

Christ also gives us the perfect model of how we, his disciples, are to love one another. He told us, "No longer do I call you servants . . . but I have called you friends" (Jn 15:5). In being our friend he has shown us how he wills us to act toward others.

We can single out several key lessons which Christ gives us about friendship:

1. *Jesus expressed and embodied God's unconditional love for us.* Jesus never cheated the disciples by giving in to the inadequate and sometimes false conditions they placed on love.

The message of the Sermon on the Mount is that we, the disciples of Jesus, are to love others *unconditionally*. We are to love others because God loves them and with the generosity with which he loves them. This may sometimes mean refusing to give in to unworthy notions of love, to acts which look loving, but which, in fact, cheat another of the possibility of discovering a deeper, more genuine form of love.

---

1. Look up the following passages. What do they tell you about Jesus' unconditional love and his call for us to love others as he has loved us?

   Mt 11:28-30   Eph 6:1-9

2. Relate the above passages to situations in daily life in which you might be asked in the name of love to do something you know to be essentially unloving. For example, what is the *truly* loving response to a friend who asks you to help him or her steal a sum of money from his parents to buy alcoholic drinks for a party?

3. Do you think that a husband and wife should challenge one another to live up to the ideals of Christian love?

To is also one B [handwritten note]

4. What about parents? Do you think that parents often find themselves having to do or say things which look unloving to their children in order to be *truly* loving to them? Give examples. Does it sometimes take courage to be loving? Explain.

Think of how parents treat each other [handwritten note]

2. *Jesus saw into people's hearts.* A child, a tax collector, a prostitute, a Samaritan woman—it made no difference. Jesus could look through the masks of guilt or fear or lack of experience or cultural differences to see into the heart of each one loved by God. His insight into others displayed in countless ways the fact that we see clearly those we truly love. Since Jesus loved with an unbounded love, he saw without difficulty into the hearts of all he met and he responded by loving them, noticing the little things that really matter. And he asked his followers to do the same. That is, he asked us to be sensitive to that glance, that tone in the voice that reveals a naked call to be loved. He asked us to look beyond external differences to discover in each one we meet someone loved by God.

ASK PARENTS IF NECESSARY

1. How does it feel when a special friend fails to be sensitive to our needs? In marriage, what are some of the "little things" that a husband and wife can do or say to communicate their sensitivity to one another?

2. Can parents usually tell when something is bothering their teenage children? Do teenagers want their parents to notice such things?

THIS IS OUT OF MY OWN EXPERIENCE

3. *Jesus was forgiving and compassionate.* While Jesus always challenged his disciples to discover and imitate God's unconditional love, at the same time he showed his disciples that this same love is essentially compassionate and forgiving. He condemned the sin but never the sinner. He saw through the masks of guilt and confusion to the *real person within,* and he spoke to that person words of healing forgiveness. The tax collector, Zacchaeus, the prostitute, Mary Magdalene, even his executioners, found themselves in the presence of forgiving love. And those who opened their hearts to receive this love found salvation in the discovery that what matters is not our weakness but the strength of God's forgiving love.

The parable of the prodigal son (Lk 15:11-12) brings home the point that Jesus asks us to love others in this same way. Like the father in the parable, we are to see not the errors of those who have wronged us but the person who, through our patience and forgiveness, might encounter in us the love and forgiveness of Christ.

1. Look up the following passages. Discuss what each reveals about Christ's forgiving love and his call for us to love others as he did.

   Lk 23:34   Mt 5:45-48   Mt 5:23-26

2. The Gospels refer to "quenching the smoking flax" and "breaking the bruised reed." Apply these images to those who are on the edge of despair because they think what they have done is too terrible to be forgiven. What is our responsibility as Christians when we meet someone in this situation?

3. Apply the following to marriage: Do you think that the intimacy of marriage inevitably reveals one's every weakness? How important is forgiveness in married love? What are some specific instances in which such forgiveness may prove to be especially difficult? Once forgiveness is given, does this place any responsibility on the one forgiven? Should it make the one who forgives feel superior to the one who has in some way failed or made a mistake? Explain your answers.

4. What are the most frequent instances in which parents need to forgive their teenage children? What are some situations in which teenagers have to forgive their parents?

---

4. *Jesus gave himself away.* Jesus did not stop at going out of his way for those around him by healing the sick or giving words of wisdom. Instead, *he gave his very life for us.* By his example he showed us that love is not safe. Loving another does not leave us intact with all our cherished possessions. Jesus tells us, his followers, that we too must carry our cross daily. We, too, must be so available, so open to those around us, that we are willing to become, in a sense, "emptied" by love. It is, in other words, by "losing" our life that we "find" it.

---

1. What do the passages listed below tell us of what Jesus taught concerning love and the gift of self?
   Eph 2:1-11   Mk 8:34-38   Jn 16:1-4

2. What are some marital situations in which a couple will of necessity have to give of themselves in order to discover the meaning of love? For starters, discuss the following: prolonged financial or health problems; career conflicts.

3. Why is parenthood inseparable from the gift of self?

Our Call to Be God's Friend

Being a Christian means more than simply observing Christ as a model upon which to base our life. It means allowing Christ to come into our life in such a way that his presence filters down into our deepest attitudes and into the way we live our daily life. When we sincerely try to follow Christ in this way, the Gospels come alive. We discover for ourselves that what Jesus did 2,000 years ago, he continues to do today in the lives of those who believe in him.

Seen in this way, there can be no better foundation for friendship and marriage than a sincerely lived Christian life. In fact, *Christian marriage* is a sacrament, a living sign of Christ's love incarnate in a husband and wife's love for one another and for their children.

SUMMARY

1. Marriage is a unique form of friendship. By understanding the basic elements of friendship, we can better understand and prepare for marriage.

2. Self-love is essential to friendship. We cannot love another unless we also love ourselves.

3. We grow in self-love through striving for goals and loving and being loved by others.

4. Loving others is essential to friendship. Loving others entails going out of our way to share in our friends' experiences.

5. A sincerely lived faith in Christ helps us to deepen our friendships and prepare for a Christian marriage.

EVALUATION

1. Write an essay on the topic of friendship as a basis for marriage. Be sure to include the themes of self-love, love of others, and a sincerely lived Christian faith.

2. Go back to the opening exercise entitled, "The Ideal

Spouse." Based upon what you have learned in this chapter, discuss as a class how the qualities of a spouse must be seen in the light of the *quality of the friendship* a husband and wife share.

BIBLE PROJECT

Gather into small groups. Each group should look up and read one of the three sets of New Testament texts listed below. In reference to each of the three texts, the group is asked to: 1) indicate what aspect or aspects of God's love for us is suggested by the text; 2) explain how a living faith in this aspect of God's love could help us in our daily life; 3) discuss how a living faith in this aspect of God's love could help a husband and wife grow in their love for one another.

Jn 4:46-54	Lk 5:12-19	Lk 11:1-11
Mt 6:31-33	Mt 5:26-30	Jn 15:1-17
Eph 2:13-22	Mk 10:46-52	Jn 10:1-18

2
Romantic-Sexual Love

You are beautiful, my beloved, ah,
you are beautiful, your eyes are doves.
—The Song of Songs

Friendship helps a marriage mature into a lasting love relationship. But most often it is romantic-sexual love, not friendship, that first moves a man and woman to become husband and wife. That is, most often a man and woman do not marry simply because they are friends, but rather because they are so deeply in love that they want to share the rest of their lives with one another. And, after the marriage takes place, it is romantic-sexual love that continues to warm the couple's friendship with a sense of mystery and renewed intimacy.

Expressing the purpose of this chapter in question form, we ask: *What aspects of romantic-sexual love lead to and foster a happy, lasting Christian marriage?* Since it is in being lovers that a husband and wife become parents, we will include in this chapter some thoughts on the role of children in marriage. To avoid repetition later on, we will not cover the full faith dimension of romantic-sexual love until we get to Chapters Three and Four, which examine marriage in the light of Scripture and church tradition.

As an opening exercise, divide into groups of either all boys or all girls. Each of the girls' groups is to make a list of 10 things a boy should do on a date, and a list of 10 things a boy should not do. The boys' groups should make a

27

similar set of lists about girls' behavior. When all are
finished, share and discuss the lists as a class.

You may want to consider the following in your discussion:

a. What are some of the similarities and differences between men and women in their respective attitudes and
expectations of the opposite sex?

b. Which of the attitudes and expectations indicated in the
exercise, carried over into marriage, would most enhance a marriage relationship? Which would threaten a
marriage relationship?

Romantic-sexual love is not an easy topic to discuss clearly,
for it covers a broad range of physical and emotional experiences,
all of which are, in a sense, unique to each person. To have a crush
on someone, to kiss, to feel sexual desire are realities we do not
know until we have experienced them. And once we experience
them, we find ourselves lost in feelings that leave us at a loss for
words to describe what we are experiencing. Nevertheless, we can
reflect upon some of the basic elements of romantic-sexual love and
how these elements affect a marriage relationship.

Personal Growth and Development

One aspect of romantic-sexual love is that it both expresses
and promotes our total growth and development as a man or
woman. To appreciate why this is so, we should keep in mind that
our sex life does not begin with puberty and adolescence, but rather
with our conception as male or female. We are sexual beings from
the moment of conception to the last moment of life. And from
childhood to old age, our masculinity or feminity deeply influences
how we think, feel, act and relate to others, as well as how others
relate to us.

The chart that follows illustrates the importance of sexual development during each stage of life. The chart is based upon Eugene
Kennedy's overview of Erik Erikson's "Eight Stages of Psychological Development" as presented in Kennedy's book, *What A Modern
Catholic Believes About Sex* (Thomas More Press, 1971).

THE EIGHT STAGES OF PSYCHOLOGICAL DEVELOPMENT

Stage	Sexual Development

Stage 1: The 1st year of life

A strong dependence on the mother or whoever takes her place. Basic capacities to give and receive love, to trust, etc., are deeply affected.

Affects later capacities to give and receive love and be intimate physically and emotionally.

Stage 2: The 2nd year of life

Child still has strong need to know he or she is loved and cared for while at the same time acquiring a healthy sense of autonomy, as, for example, in first awareness of the body apart from the mother's body; ability to make conscious movements, etc.

Affects later ability to accept presence of sexual urges and yet to control these urges and bring sexual desires under the influence of reason and ideals.

Stage 3: Ages 3 to 6

Child continues to have strong need for security of parents' love and to expand yet further his or her autonomy in the ability to set and achieve goals.

Growing self-acceptance with accompanying self-control. How parents respond to child's sexual curiosity about the body, to masturbation, etc., affects later attitudes.

Stage 4: Six to puberty

Child's world expands to neighborhood and school. Child learns to accomplish tasks more independently of parents.

Child becomes aware of how parents relate to one another, how they show affection for each other, and together show affection for child. Child works at acquiring sense of confidence in his or her emerging sexual identity.

Stage 5: Adolescence

Dynamic, rapid physical and emotional change and growth. Strong need to develop an identity as an adult rather than a child. Peers and models of behavior help direct growth.

Crucial questions of past experiences, masturbation, premarital sex affect ability for continued growth. Need to establish ideals and attitudes concerning sexual identity and how to properly express it.

Stage 6: Young adult

New, more adult situations in which to continue testing and forming identity and ideals. Moves either closer to or further away from others.

All that has gone before is crucial in helping to establish responsible, mature and independent attitudes toward sexual behavior and love relationships in general.

Stage 7: Young and middle adult

Enters responsible love relationship. Acquires a sense of values, of family and children.

The person begins to acquire a sensitivity to the relationship between sexual activity and responsibility for others.

Stage 8: Later adult

Time for reflection, for summing up one's life.

Time to acknowledge mistakes, to see sexuality in terms of one's integrity and dignity as a person.

After reading through the chart and sharing initial observations, respond to the following questions:

1. What are some specific examples of ways adolescent and adult sexual attitudes and behavior are shaped by childhood experiences? What does this suggest about the long-term role that parents play in their children's lives?

2. How can childhood experiences influence one's later ability to have a happy, lasting marriage? How can sexual attitudes and behavior in adolescence influence later marital happiness?

3. In relating the chart to the material on self-love in Chapter One, why is our sexuality an integral part of our sense of self-worth and dignity as a person?

The Worth of Love

There is a marriage counselor who keeps a poster hanging in her office which reads, "Love is a hell of a lot of work." No doubt the couples who come into her office are well aware of the truth of this statement. In fact, any couple who has been married very long knows that love is a lot of many things. It is a lot of happiness, excitement, and fulfillment. But it is also, at times, a lot of work.

The work of love is the mutual effort required to remain sensitive, open and concerned about each other's deepest feelings and needs. When love is present, we intend to be sensitive and concerned about the needs of others. Between lovers, it is possible that not even a glance or a touch of the hand goes unnoticed. When love is present, sexual desires and romantic feelings serve to intensify the couple's intimacy. By making love, a husband and wife fulfill their desire to belong completely to one another.

But love is not always present. The completely loving man or woman is the ideal rather than the reality. We are each both loving and unloving. For the most part, we want to be loving and often are. Yet, at times, we miss the ideal. At times we choose to satisfy our own needs or cater to our own emotions, even when this means being insensitive or even hurtful to those we love. Our sexuality participates in this selfishness, for the genital-emotional pleasures associated with sexual experiences make these experiences especially susceptible to selfishness. Without love, sexual desires and romantic impulses leave two people isolated in the pursuit of physical or emotional gratification. With the passage of time, this exploitation turns into indifference, as each becomes bored with a sexual routine devoid of love.

Considering that each of us is a "mixed bag" of loving and unloving possibilities, it is understandable that every marriage has its ups and downs. Every couple experiences something of both the joy of mutual love and the sorrow that follows failures in love.

But this does not mean that we are at the mercy of each unpredictable moment. *For we can choose love.* We can choose to work at caring about others as much as we do ourselves. When two people get married, they make a solemn promise to engage in the work of love together. They vow to live for each other's happiness. As lovers, they vow to fill their sexuality with love. They vow, that is, to be a loving man or woman, someone sensitive and caring about every aspect of their spouse's happiness.

As the chart given earlier suggests, the capacity to integrate our sexuality into a responsible love relationship is the mark of the mature adult. In getting married, a man and woman solemnly vow to become one another's source of this growth and integration. Love is hard work. But by faithfully working together to make love the foundation of their lives, a couple can reap the reward of a lifetime of happiness as husband and wife.

1. Applying what was said above to the high school years, think of a specific incident illustrating how being loving toward each of the following can, at times, be hard work.

   - a younger brother or sister
   - an older brother or sister
   - a parent
   - a classmate
   - a teacher
   - a boyfriend or girlfriend

2. After sharing your responses, discuss the following: How does a person's reaction to such incidents reveal his or her level of maturity? What was an occasion on which you depended on one of the above to be loving toward you when you were behaving in an unloving way?

Is It the Real Thing?

From about the senior year of high school, any serious, lasting romantic relationship leads a couple to at least consider marriage. But how can a couple tell if the way they feel about each other is an indication that they should get married? There is no "surefire" answer to this question. We can, however, briefly list some considerations that can help a couple arrive at a decision.

Maturity:

Do both partners have the maturity required to make a final commitment? Are they both old enough to have a basic awareness of themselves as adults who know their goals, their strengths, weaknesses, etc.?

How old do you think people have to be before they can truly fall in love? How old before they are ready to get married?

Know each other:

Has the couple dated long enough to know each other well enough to get married? Have they frankly discussed religion, how many children they would like to have, future goals, etc.? Are they aware of tendencies such as moodiness, violent temper, excessive drinking, etc., that may prove to be very troublesome later on?

What do you think is the minimum time a couple should know each other before getting married? Make a list of 10 topics you think a couple should discuss frankly before marriage.

Family background:

Will there be big adjustments to make because of differences in family background? For example, are there differences in financial status, religion, family size, etc.? Are there differences in the atmosphere in the home, such as one family being very strict and the other very easygoing?

---

1) How big a role do you think in-laws play in a marriage?
2) Do you think each partner in a marriage consciously or unconsciously brings the attitudes and values of his or her family into the marriage?

Goals:

Are the partners' goals compatible? Will getting married at this time prevent one or both partners from reaching some cherished goal, such as finishing college, traveling or living independently?

How important is it for a husband and wife to share or support one another's goals? For example, if they wish, is it important for both of them to finish college before getting married? Is it realistic for a couple to marry and still finish their education?

Freedom:

Is the decision to marry free from pressures influencing one or both partners to feel they have to get married? That is, will the pronouncing of the marriage vows be a truly free act for which both partners can assume full responsibility?

Do you think it is wise for a couple to get married because the girl is pregnant? What are some other factors that would make a couple feel pressured to get married?

Love:

Is the love the couple shares so total, so deep, so basic that they will be willing to go to great lengths to preserve it and enhance its growth?

Do you think a couple somehow know when their love is
genuine? Can two people who are truly in love fall out of
love? If so, how can this happen?

Sexual Intimacy in Marriage

After the wedding ceremony and reception, the bride and
groom usually waste little time in leaving for their honeymoon. The
anticipation and perhaps some degree of uneasiness preceding the
honeymoon as well as the memories it leaves illustrate the importance of sexual intimacy in marriage. But the question we ask here
is: How does the experience of sexual intimacy change and evolve
over a lifetime of living together as husband and wife? What is
the significance of sexual intimacy after five, 10, or 30 years of
marriage?

There are as many answers to these questions as there are married couples. Just as every marriage relationship is unique, so too
is the sexual intimacy that each couple shares. And yet it is possible to make some general observations about an overall pattern
that is, in one way or another, applicable to most marriages.
Though significantly changed to suit our present needs, the following material is based upon three distinct phases of marriage as
developed by Paul Tournier in his book *To Understand Each Other*
(John Knox Press, 1967).

1. *The Romance Stage.* During the romance or honeymoon
phase, a couple feel they are able to communicate easily. They
love to be together. And they seem to never run out of things to
talk about and share with one another. The conflicts they experience are of little consequence in light of the joy they have in making up afterward. Since sex is a form of communication, sexual
intimacy at this stage expresses the passion and the romance of
their relationship.

2. *The disillusionment stage,* which often comes to a head
between the fifth and 10th years of marriage, results from the wear-

ing away of the initial, idealized and always somewhat false image that lovers first have of one another. Such disillusionment is inevitable. When two people share one bed, one table, one everything, they begin to become keenly aware of each other's faults and failings. Besides this, they may begin to feel the excitement and newness of their marriage are gradually being replaced by a dull daily routine and a tendency to take each other for granted. Sometimes, too, serious conflicts can surface which seem impossible to resolve. In short, as the saying has it, "The honeymoon is over."

During the stage of disillusionment, a couple may take one of three paths: a) *Divorce or separation*. Convinced that they can never resolve their differences, the couple may decide to terminate the marriage. b) *Living together yet apart*. The couple may take a path of marital detente, each tolerating, yet never truly listening to the other. They continue to love one another, but do so in the midst of major unresolved tensions or misunderstandings. In such a situation, sexual intimacy may be a bittersweet experience. Sexual encounters may express a union they both desire, yet somehow seem unable to reach due to a deep-seated emotional divorce that leaves them unable to communicate at a level that makes sexual intimacy meaningful. c) *Mature love*. The third path leading out of marital disillusionment is that of mature love, which constitutes the third phase of marriage. *Mature love* is characterized by both partners searching together for a love capable of embracing and uniting them in their differences. As this love is reached, the couple continues to experience ups and downs in its relationship. But, at the same time, there is a genuine growth in being able to accept, appreciate, and understand each other in a more stable and lasting way.

The couple's sexual intimacy at this stage continues to be expressed in many different ways. There are moments of passion and casual tenderness, as well as moments of misunderstanding. But the couple's sexual encounters begin to take on the richness and the depth of the love they share. If put into words, each might say: This person whom I love so much, who knows me so well, who has shared so much with me and sacrificed so much for me, is now one with me as we express our love for one another.

An analogy can be made to a man and woman eating a meal together. Eating a meal can be a *purely physical act*. A man and woman can sit together at one table as strangers, *each satisfying his or her hunger* for food. When carried out in this way, a meal communicates nothing of the human qualities that make us essentially different from animals, which also seek to gratify their need for food.

In contrast to this purely physical act of eating, a man and woman can share an intimate meal together. At such a meal, the act of eating remains a physical act. Yet the eating is at the same time *more* than that. The shared meal has the potential of becoming an act of love. The eating of the meal expresses the body's ability to communicate interior attitudes of love and concern for another person. Here, the meal takes on the dimensions of a special occasion, a time the couple will long remember as a precious moment of shared love and closeness to one another.

---

1. Imagine a married couple having an intimate meal as a way of celebrating their 10th wedding anniversary. Discuss how each of the items listed below might be an important aspect of the couple's evening together.

- Being fully present to one another

- Being open, sincere and honest

- Putting all other concerns aside

- Sharing memories of past experiences together

- Sharing hopes for future happiness

- Saying, "I love you"

- Sharing silence

- Embracing and holding one another

- Being patient and understanding when one fails to meet the other's expectations

    Why would sexual intercourse be especially appropriate on such an evening? Go back over the above items referring to the couple's shared meal and indicate how each might play an important part in the couple's sexual intimacy.

2. Discuss how taking a walk together, working together on a common task, being open about honest disagreements, caring for each other or one of the children

in illness, etc., are all ways of making love more present and meaningful in marriage.

3. Compare the *meaning* and significance of sexual intercourse as discussed above with sexual intercourse in each of the following situations: a) a prostitute with her customer; b) two high school freshmen who have sex together because they "really love each other"; c) a girl who agrees to have sex with her boyfriend who insists she "prove" her love for him.

4. The church teaches that sexual intercourse and all acts leading directly to it are morally good only within marriage. Discuss this moral teaching in the light of the following: a) responsibility for our sexuality; b) relationship of sexual activity to personal growth; c) capacity for sexual intercourse to express a total love commitment; and d) the effectiveness of the church in directing young people's attitudes and behavior in the area of sexuality.

Becoming Parents

Parenthood is built into the very essence of married love, for a baby is the natural outcome of the couple's sexual expressions of love. Unless a husband and wife practice some form of birth control or there is a medical problem of some kind, their repeated sexual encounters will ordinarily result in pregnancy and the birth of a child.

Children play a potentially constructive role in a couple's growth toward mature love. During the first few years of marriage, a child can help a couple become more aware of the life-giving dimensions of their love. A child can also help a couple realize the extent and nature of the responsibilities they took upon themselves in getting married. Later, during periods of disillusionment, children can help a couple understand the importance of doing everything in their power to make their marriage work to provide a loving, stable environment for their children. And in reaching some degree of mature love, a couple can hardly avoid being brought closer together through the love they share for their children as they watch them grow and develop and learn to return to their parents the love they have received.

Of course, parenthood involves risks and challenges of its own. Each stage of a child's life brings to the parents not only new blessings, but also new concerns and responsibilities. In getting married the husband and wife agree to face these rewards and challenges together. Their wedding vows amount to an act of hope that through loving one another they will grow together with their children to become mature people who love and care about others in spite of failings and difficulties.

In small groups indicate what you think are the burdens and rewards of parenthood during each stage of a child's life as listed below. Where appropriate, indicate how these burdens and rewards differ with respect to the husband and the wife.

	Burdens	Rewards
• planning for the first child	——————	——————
• pregnancy	——————	——————
• infancy/toddler	——————	——————
• grade school	——————	——————
• junior high/preteen	——————	——————
• teenager	——————	——————
• young adult leaving home	——————	——————
• adult living on his or her own	——————	——————

Romantic-sexual Love in a Christian Marriage

A Christian marriage is an ordinary marriage in which both spouses share a sincere desire to make Christ the center of their lives. And this, in part, means they desire to love one another as Christ has loved them and as he continues to love them in and through their love for each other and for their children.

John Powell in his book *Unconditional Love* (Argus Communications, 1978), beautifully clarifies the nature of Christ's love upon which Christians base their lives. By adapting Powell's insights to our present needs, we can see the positive contribution that Christian faith makes in a married couple's romantic-sexual love.

Our reflections are based upon Luke's account of Christ's temptation in the desert, which reads as follows:

> Jesus, full of the Holy Spirit, then returned to the Jordan and was conducted by the Spirit into the desert for 40 days, where he was tempted by the devil. During that time he ate nothing, and at the end of it he was hungry. The devil said to him, "If you are the Son of God, command this stone to turn into bread." Jesus answered him, "Scripture has it, 'Not on bread alone shall man live.' " Then the devil took him up higher and showed him all the kingdoms of the world in a single instant. He said to him, "I will give you all this power and the glory of these kingdoms; the power has been given to me and I give it to whomever I wish. Prostrate yourself in homage before me, and it shall all be yours." In reply, Jesus said to him, "Scripture has it,
>
> > 'You shall do homage to the Lord
> > your God;
> > him alone shall you adore.' "
>
> Then the devil led him to Jerusalem, set him on the parapet of the temple, and said to him, "If you are the Son of God, throw yourself down from here, for Scripture has it,
>
> > 'He will bid his angels watch over you';
> > > and again,
> > 'With their hands they will support you, that you may never stumble on a stone.' "
>
> Jesus said to him in reply, "It also says,
> 'You shall not put the Lord your God to the test.' "
> When the devil had finished all the tempting, he left him, to await another opportunity.
>
> (Lk 4:1-13)

In the first temptation, that of turning stones into bread, Jesus reveals to us that we, his followers, are not to base our lives on satisfying mere bodily desires. A Christlike love is not a love of pleasure for pleasure's sake. In the second temptation, that of gaining worldly power, Jesus reveals that we are not to base our lives on gaining power over others. A Christlike love is not a love of power. And in the third temptation, that of leaping off the roof of the temple, Jesus reveals to us that we, his followers, are not to abdicate our responsibility for our actions. A Christlike love is not careless with the responsibility that one assumes in being an adult.

In a Christian marriage, a man and woman pray and work together to integrate Christ's love into every aspect of their daily lives. As a part of this totality, their romantic-sexual encounters are diverted toward the highest ideal of love as revealed by Christ.

In such a love, each tells the other in effect: We will not base our romantic-sexual intimacy on pleasure alone. We will not use sex as a way of gaining power over each other; exploitation and manipulation will have no place in our sexual intimacies. Together we accept the full responsibility of our love. We will not expose ourselves to situations of marital infidelity. We will remain true to the commitments we have made and to the full life-giving potential of our sexual union.

Christian faith then gives meaning and direction to a married couple's romantic-sexual love. It gives them the highest possible ideal upon which to pattern their love; namely, the love of Christ, which is the greatest love the world has ever known. For, as we saw at the end of Chapter I, Christ's love is, in fact, God's love. It is an *unconditional love* that knows neither beginning nor end.

When and if you decide to marry, do you think sharing your Christian faith with your spouse will be important to you? What are some of the ways in which Christian couples share their faith?

Do you think that a married couple's romantic-sexual love will tend to drift or weaken if it is not directed toward an ideal or goal?

How Far Can You Go?

It is inevitable that a religiously orientated discussion of romantic-sexual love directed to teenagers and young adults gives rise to the question: How far can you go? That is, at what point is sexual intimacy outside of marriage morally wrong?

How one answers this question will be greatly affected by his or her principles of right and wrong as well as his or her understanding of the nature of human love and sexuality. And so we refine our question and ask: How far can you go if you are someone who is trying to live a good Christian life? At what point does sexual intimacy before marriage run contrary to the teaching of Christ?

In one sense, sexual intimacy before marriage begins to be immoral at the same point at which it can become immoral in marriage—when it ceases to be a genuine act of human love. It is in being insensitive, hurtful, or in some way selfish that sexual intimacies in or out of marriage fail to live up to the ideal of Christlike love.

A second and equally important approach is based upon the Christian teaching that sexual intercourse and all acts leading directly to it form a unique expression of human intimacy in that intercourse expresses a *total* gift of self and the possibility of creating new life. When a married couple have sexual intercourse in a caring and loving way, they express with their bodies the reality of their lives. They are one. Thus for them "to go all the way" physically through sexual intercourse corresponds to the truth of their lives. Furthermore, a married couple's commitment to one another means that they accept the responsibility to care for and love the children that will result from their sexual union.

So, in responding to the question How far can you go? we can respond by saying: Go as far as love demands. Let every embrace and kiss and sign of affection express a genuine mutual affection and concern for one another. And going as far as love demands with respect to intercourse means to refrain from intercourse as a way of respecting one another's future capacity to give *totally* through sexual intercourse in marriage.

1. What are some ways other than sexual intimacy that a couple can use to express affection for one another?

2. Is there still a double standard for sexual experiences— one set of "acceptable" behaviors for boys and a different set for girls? Does this double standard come from society or the church?

3. Do most parents know how much sexual activity is going on among high school couples, or are they ignorant of such things? What are some parental rules about being alone, a time to be home from a date, etc., that reflect common sense about these matters? What rules are unfair?

SUMMARY

1. Romantic-sexual love both expresses and promotes our total growth and development as a man or woman.

2. If a marriage is to be successful, a husband and wife must involve themselves in the "hard work" of maintaining a sensitive, open and concerned love for each other.

3. The decision to get married calls for mature consideration of a number of factors.

4. Sexual intimacy in marriage reflects the depth and maturity of the love the couple shares.

5. Parenthood is built into the very essence of married love.

6. Christian faith gives meaning and direction to a married couple's romantic-sexual love by establishing Christ's love as its goal.

7. Before marriage, a couple's expressions of affection should all be genuinely loving and sensitive to each other's dignity as persons. Sexual intercourse is a unique form of human intimacy that is intended by God to be used only in the total commitment of marriage.

EVALUATION

Write seven well-developed paragraphs discussing each of the seven summary points listed above.

CREATIVE PROJECT

Divide into small groups and research attitudes toward romantic-sexual love as expressed by the mass media. After all the groups have had time to do their research, report the findings to the class.

Some of the areas for research are:

- Prime time television shows
- Soap operas
- Rock music lyrics
- Magazines
- Movies

GUEST SPEAKERS

Invite one or more married couples to speak to the class about what they have found to be important to the happiness of their marriage.

3
Marriage in Scripture

*For this reason a man shall leave
his father and mother, and shall
cling to his wife, and the two
shall be made into one.*

—Genesis

Chapters One and Two made reference to the Christian faith dimension of marriage. In this chapter we turn our full attention to what Scripture reveals to us about the place of marriage in God's plan for our salvation.

Marriage in the Old Testament

The first two chapters of the Book of Genesis consist of two different creation accounts, each of which contains its own revelations about the nature and purpose of marriage. The first account (Gn 1:1-2:4a) is commonly referred to as the Priestly account. This text presents the creation of Adam and Eve as the crowning event of the six days of God's creation:

> Then God said: "Let us make man in our image, after our likeness. Let them have dominion over the fish of the sea, the birds of the air, and the cattle, and over all the wild animals and all the creatures that crawl on the ground."

God created man in his image;
in the divine image he created him;
male and female he created them.

God blessed them, saying: "Be fertile and multiply;
fill the earth and subdue it. Have dominion over the
fish of the sea, the birds of the air, and all the living
things that move on the earth." God also said: "See,
I give you every seed-bearing plant all over the earth
and every tree that has seed-bearing fruit on it to be
your food; and to all the animals of the land, all the
birds of the air, and all the living creatures that
crawl on the ground, I give all the green plants for
food." And so it happened. God looked at everything he had made, and he found it very good. . . .
                                        (Gn 1:26-31)

The second creation account (Gn 2:4b-25) is often known
as the Yahwist account. This second account does not begin with
a watery chaos, as does the Priestly account. Instead, we are told
of a barren desert through which flows a river. On the shores of
this river God forms Adam "out of the clay of the ground" (Gn
2:7). God then prepares a beautiful garden for Adam to inhabit
and cultivate. The text goes on to state:

The LORD God said: "It is not good for the
man to be alone. I will make a suitable partner for
him."
So the LORD God cast a deep sleep on the
man, and while he was asleep, he took out one of
his ribs and closed up its place with flesh. The
LORD God then built up into a woman the rib that
he had taken from the man. When he brought her
to the man, the man said:
"This one, at last, is bone of my bones
and flesh of my flesh;
This one shall be called 'woman,'
for out of 'her man' this one has been taken."
That is why a man leaves his father and mother and
clings to his wife, and the two of them become one
body. The man and his wife were both naked, yet
they felt no shame.   (Gn 2:18, 21-25)

Marriage and Family Life

The two texts cited above allow us to make some observations about the Old Testament teaching on marriage. Turning first to the Priestly account, we find that the union of husband and wife is directly linked with the command to "be fertile and multiply." In other words, the responsibility and privilege of having children is inseparable from God's plan in creating us as male and female.

The Jews were sensitive to the central role that children play in married love (Ru 4:13; 1 Sm 1:1-9). In fact, children were considered to be so basic to marriage that not having children was something of a curse (1 Sm 1:5-6; Hos 9:11-14). It meant being "blotted out of Israel" (Dt 25:6).

This tradition underscores the dignity given by the Jews to women. A woman's dignity was closely linked to her ability to bear children. Furthermore, the woman of the house held a position of singular honor in the home in her role as the primary teacher of the children (Prv 1:8; 4:1; 6:20; 23:22-25).

---

1. How did the insistence upon the relationship of sexual intimacy and children help to foster and protect the unity of family life for the Old Testament Jews?

2. What attitudes in our society today do you feel are in opposition to this family-oriented attitude toward sexual intimacy found in the Old Testament?

3. Do you personally agree that the dignity of a woman rests in her role as wife and mother? Do you think the wife should be the "heart of the home"? In what way would you add to or alter this notion of feminine dignity?

The Love Between Husband and Wife

The strong emphasis placed by the Priestly account of creation on having children did not exclude the importance of romantic love in marriage. As the Yahwist account makes clear, a husband and wife's sexual union is not *solely* for the purpose of begetting children. In fact, the second creation account puts the union between husband and wife purely within the context of partners who cling to one another as "one body," who are naked and "yet feel no shame."

Though somewhat subdued and in the background, this aspect of loving intimacy in marriage is mentioned often in the Old Testament. For example, when Hannah, wife of Elkanah, complains to her husband that he has given her no children, he responds, "Am I not worth more to you than 10 sons?" (1 Sm 1:5-8). We find, too, that Jacob worked for seven years to marry Rachel instead of paying the traditional marriage dowry in money. And we are told that the seven years "seemed to him like but a few days because of his love for her" (Gn 29:20). The Book of Deuteronomy states that when a young man married, he was to be free from all public duties for one full year following the wedding to allow him to "be happy with his wife."

It is significant that as time went on, the Jews came to see value even in a childless marriage. What mattered most to God

was not a large family, but rather the fertility of a life of virtue and fidelity to him (Sir 26:1-3; Wis 3:13-15; Is 56:5).

Finally, the Old Testament held the romantic dimension of marriage in such high esteem that it was presented as a sign of the covenant of love between Yahweh and Israel. In these texts the Lord is a divine lover and Israel is his bride (Sg; Hos 3:1-5; Is 54:4-8; Jer 2:2-37).

In looking at both the Priestly and Yahwist accounts, we see that *both* sexual union without openness to children and parenthood without romantic love fall short of what God intends marriage to be. This divine affirmation of romantic love and children provided the bases upon which the Jews recognized the value and meaning of married love. The whole of the Song of Songs is based upon the holiness of sexual love for its own sake:

Let him kiss me with kisses of his mouth!
More delightful is your love than wine!
    Your name spoken is a spreading perfume—
    that is why the maidens love you.
Draw me!—
    We will follow you eagerly!
Bring me, O king, to your chambers.
With you we rejoice and exult, we extol your love;
    it is beyond wine:
  how rightly you are loved!

*   *   *

My lover speaks; he says to me,
    "Arise, my beloved, my beautiful one,
    and come"
 For see, the winter is past,
    the rains are over and gone.
The flowers appear on the earth,
    the time of pruning the vines has come,
    and the song of the dove is heard in our land.

*   *   *

On my bed at night I sought him whom my heart loves—
                    (Sg 1:2-4; 2:10-12; 3:1)

1. Discuss as a class whether or not you agree that the best thing a husband and wife can do for their children is to deepen their love for each other.

2. Do you feel even relatively small children are able to sense whether or not their parents are truly close and loving toward one another? What influence does this have on their own emotional growth and development?

Marriage Shares in the Holiness of Creation

The revelation that all creation is given by God and proclaimed by him to be good caused the Jews to see the goodness and presence of God in the ordinary events of daily life. Such common activities as talking with a friend, eating a meal, and going to sleep at night were seen to be holy events in which the Jew experienced the goodness and nearness of God.

Similarly, marriage was seen to be holy. God himself created marriage "in the beginning." God himself decreed, "It is not good for the man to be alone" (Gn 2:18). By the will of God a man and woman are to live together as husband and wife.

The Jew's belief in the natural goodness of marriage is demonstrated in the marriage customs of Old Testament times. As was the custom of other cultures at this time, a Jewish wedding was arranged by the parents, who chose a suitable partner for their son or daughter.

For most of us today the custom of parents choosing their children's marriage partners may seem a bit strange. The custom becomes more understandable, however, in light of the evidence that the parents most often considered the feelings of their children in this matter (Gn 24:8, 58). There is also evidence that the children were not always docile in accepting their parents' choice of a partner (Gn 24:37-40). It is also worth noting that during this time the bride was to be no younger than 12 and the groom no younger than 13 when they married. At such a young age a decisive role of the parents was almost unavoidable, if not outright necessary.

With the arrangements for the marriage completed, the time of the *betrothal* began. During this time, the young couple was considered to be fully committed to the marriage, even though they did not live together as husband and wife. The betrothal ended with the groom giving the father of the bride the *mohar* or dowry sum of money (Gn 24:53; Ex 22:16).

The ceremony itself consisted of little more than a procession of the bride to the bridegroom's home, where the father of the groom accepted the bride as his own child. During the procession wedding hymns were sung (Ps 45). The wedding festivities lasted a full week, and they included a great deal of feasting and drinking.

Interestingly enough, the marriage customs did not in any way involve the temple or synagogue. Until very late (14 B.C.) priests had no connections with the marriage ceremony. At that time marriage was not so much a religious affair. It was a family affair in which the Jew was to experience the goodness and love of God. By entering into marriage, the Jew was to see his or her spouse and children as meeting places with the daily presence of God's love and goodness.

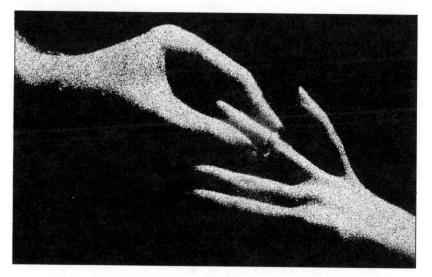

Within the Old Testament vision of the world created and held in existence by God, everything in the world is seen as a gift revealing aspects of God's love for us. The mountains, for example, reveal that God's love for us is strong and eternal. The coming of spring reveals that his love brings us new life. Similarly, marriage, being created by God, also expresses and makes present aspects of God's love for us.

Listed below are some important moments or events that occur in marriage. Gather into small groups and propose two or three adjectives or phrases that you think describe the kind of love each item expresses. Secondly, after each of your responses, indicate how the adjective or descriptive phrase can be applied to God's love for us. When all are finished, share and discuss your responses as a class.

- the honeymoon

- a mother nursing her baby

- parents teaching their child to take its first step

- forgiving a spouse for a wrong done

- caring for one another in sickness

- being faithful to one another until death

Marriage Shares in the Mystery of Evil

The Jews' conviction of the basic goodness of marriage did not blind them to the many difficulties and sorrows which are part of every marriage. For the Jews this negative aspect of marriage finds its origin in the sin of our first parents, as revealed in chapters two and three of the Book of Genesis.

These chapters of Genesis tell us that marriage shares in the effects of sin. This note of sadness or difficulty in marriage, however, is immediately followed by the hope resulting from God's promise that the woman's offspring would crush the power of evil (Gn 3:15). This hope is reinforced in the call of Abraham and the giving of the Covenant to Moses. It was in following God's call and remaining faithful to his Covenant love that the Jewish married couple found love and strength in the sometimes dark and tumultuous areas of married life.

Listed below are some of the ways that, according to the Old Testament, original sin has affected marriage. Gather into small groups and think of two or three specific ways that each harmful act or attitude can be expressed in the lives of married couples today.

1) The act of putting on fig leaves (Gn 3:7) which can symbolize a couple concealing their innermost feelings from one another.

2) After the fall, God decreed to the woman that "He shall be your master" (Gn 3:16), which can symbolize a man dominating a woman instead of caring for her.

3) In the story of the fall, Adam tried to shift the blame to Eve (Gn 3:12), which can symbolize how husbands and wives can shift their responsibilities instead of trusting and working with one another.

Both husbands and wives must face the possibility of watching their children grow up to hurt and be hurt by others, as suggested in the story of Cain and Abel (Gn 4:1-16).

After sharing your responses as a class, discuss together how a shared faith in God's love for them could help a couple face and overcome each of the above situations.

The New Testament Teaching on Marriage

Much of the New Testament teaching on marriage finds its basis in the Old Testament. For example, Jesus quotes the Old Testament in affirming the divine origins of marriage (Mt 19:3-5). And Saint Paul exhorts Christians to uphold the Old Testament values of a home in which the family members love and respect one another (Eph 6:1-4). We can note, too, that marriage for the early

Christians continued to be a family affair, celebrated in the house as a natural, God-given part of daily life.

What is new, however, in the New Testament teaching on marriage is the *new meaning* given to marriage, derived from the new meaning Christ has given to human love. This new meaning is beautifully expressed in the first letter of John:

> Beloved,
> let us love one another
> because love is of God;
> everyone who loves is begotten of God
> and has knowledge of God.
> The man without love has known nothing of God,
> for God is love.
> God's love was revealed in our midst in this way:
> he sent his only Son to the world
> that we might have life through him.
> Love, then, consists in this:
> not that we have loved God,
> but that he has loved us
> and has sent his Son as an offering for our sins.
> Beloved,
> if God has loved us so,
> we must have the same love for one another.
> No one has ever seen God.
> Yet if we love one another
> God dwells in us,
> and his love is brought to perfection in us.
>
>   *　　*　　*
>
> When anyone acknowledges that
>   Jesus is the Son of God,
> God dwells in him
> and he in God.
> We have come to know and to believe
>   in the love God has for us.
> God is love,
> and he who abides in love
> abides in God,
> and God in him.

(1 Jn 4:7-12, 15-16)

The above passage provides us with a focal point for presenting the place of marriage in Christian life.

God is love forever expressed as Father, Son and Holy Spirit. We are creatures of God's love. More, we are God's children called by God to share perfectly in his eternal life of love. In creating us as persons in his image and likeness, God the Father calls us to perfect union with himself through Christ the Word (1 Jn 2:3-6).

Our sin is our free refusal to love God. Lost in sin, we are exiled from God's love, which is our life and our happiness. But God loved us first. He has revealed his boundless love for us, for the Father has sent the Son to become one with us in order to heal our sins by dying on the cross and rising from the dead.

Now we who believe in Jesus and follow him as his disciples have eternal life in him. We are carried by him into the bosom of the Father. Our eternal life in Christ begins with baptism when the Holy Spirit unites us to Christ. And we celebrate our eternal life in Christ in sharing together in the love feast (agape) of the Eucharist (Jn 6:25-40). But above all of this, Christ has made our love for one another to be the measure of our love for him. It is in loving one another as Christ has loved us that we fulfill the commandment of the Lord:

> "As the Father has loved me,
> so I have loved you.
> Live on in my love
> You will live in my love
> if you keep my commandments, . . .

> "This is my commandment:
> love one another
> as I have loved you.

> "The command I give you is this,
> that you love one another."

> (Jn 15:9-10, 12, 17;
> see also 1 Jn 4:20-21)

Saint Paul provides us with the connective link between Christian love and marriage. He writes, "Husbands, love your wives, as Christ loved the church" (Eph 5:25). And in this same passage he continues to speak of the union of husband and wife, "This is a great mystery. I mean in reference to Christ and to the church" (Eph 5:32, CCD Edition).

In a Christian marriage the husband and wife become one another's primary meeting place with Christ, who lives in them and in whom they are one. It is in loving each other as Christ has loved them that they find in each other the means to their mutual union with God.

This union in Christ is not a matter of pious thoughts. Rather, it is the faith dimension of the everyday events of a normal marriage between a man and woman who seek to express their love for Christ through their love for one another and their children:

A child gets an "A" on a test. Another child is ill. The wife prepares her husband's favorite dessert. The husband gets up Saturday morning with the children so his wife can sleep in. Or the husband and wife make sure they get away together alone for a special weekend in which to renew their love for each other. When lived out in an attitude of sincere faith, such experiences enable the husband, wife and children to experience and give witness to the love of Christ present in our daily lives.

Indeed, the experience of married love in the Christian home serves to remind the whole church that when we say, "the Word became flesh and made his dwelling among us" (Jn 1:14), we imply that God has loved us to the point of identifying our life with his own. He has come to share in and wait for us in the midst of our daily lives (1 Jn).

Marriage is a "great mystery," for a Christian couple's union with one another participates in and expresses the life-giving union between ourselves and Christ. In every embrace and touch and shared experience Christian couples in some way are embraced and touched by Christ, whose presence they are invited to experience in their love for one another.

---

1. Listed below are a number of basic human needs and experiences. First, go through the list individually and indicate how being deeply in love with someone would contribute to each item listed. When finished, try to add ideas of your own to the list.

   - finding meaning in life

   - having the courage to face a major crisis or disappointment

   - realizing one's worth as a person

   - knowing by experience that it truly is better to give than to receive, that is, knowing the importance of overcoming selfishness

   - overcoming loneliness

2. After finishing the above, gather into small groups. Compare your answers. Then, working together, indicate how a personal love for our Lord could also help someone in each of the ways listed.

3. Finally, share the responses as a class. In conclusion, imagine that you have found someone with whom you are deeply in love and with whom you can share and grow in your faith in Christ. What does this suggest about the personal growth and fulfillment that are possible in a Christian marriage?

The Permanence of Marriage

At the time of Jesus there was a debate among the rabbis over the question of divorce. The Mosaic law allowed a man to divorce his wife if he found "something indecent" in her (Dt 24: 1-4). But the rabbis had conflicting notions about what precisely constituted "something indecent." On the stricter side of the debate, headed by Rabbi Hillel, indecency consisted of adultery or some other equally scandalous act. In opposition to this position, Rabbi Shammai and his followers taught that indecency applied to such trivial shortcomings as the wife's bad cooking.

One day the Pharisees approached Jesus to see where he stood on the question of divorce:

> Then some Pharisees came up and as a test began to ask him whether it was permissible for a husband to divorce his wife. In reply he said, "What command did Moses give you?" They answered, "Moses permitted divorce and the writing of a decree of divorce." But Jesus told them: "He wrote that commandment for you because of your stubbornness. At the beginning of creation God made them male and female; for this reason a man shall leave his father and mother and the two shall become as one. They are no longer two but one flesh. Therefore let no man separate what God has joined." Back in the house again, the disciples began to question him about this. He told them, "Whoever divorces his wife and marries another commits adultery against her; and the woman who divorces her husband and marries another commits adultery."
>
> (Mk 10:2-12)

Jesus' response is a quantum leap not only beyond the debate of the rabbis, but beyond the Law of Moses itself. In effect, Jesus says that there are no grounds for divorce. Using God's Word spoken in creation as his authority, he teaches that his followers who marry are bound as "one flesh" in a union which no man is to separate. In the eyes of God marriage is absolute and final, ended only by death. The response of the disciples to Jesus serves to illustrate the unconditional nature of Jesus' condemnation of divorce. They said, "If that is the case between man and wife, it is better not to marry" (Mt 19:10).

There is a direct relationship between Jesus' teaching on divorce and the "great mystery" by which marital love shares in the love between Christ and ourselves. In effect, Christ is telling his disciples: When you who are my disciples marry, your love for each other participates in and expresses my love for you. And so your love must be as undying as the love I revealed to you in my death and resurrection. Just as you and I are inseparably united in my love, so too, you as husband and wife are inseparably united in my love.

Two Exceptions?

There are two New Testament texts which appear to weaken Jesus' condemnation of divorce. One of these texts appears in Matthew's Gospel, in which a clause is added to the statement on divorce from Mark's Gospel. The text as it appears in Matthew reads, "I now say to you, whoever divorces his wife (lewd conduct is a separate case) and marries another commits adultery, and the man who marries a divorced woman commits adultery" (Mt 19:9-10).

This reference to lewd conduct has been the focal point of much debate. For many Protestant theologians and some biblical scholars, the text suggests that Jesus' condemnation of divorce refers to the permanence of marriage as an ideal open to exceptions which permit divorce. Other biblical scholars and Catholic theologians, however, hold that this passage about lewd conduct upholds Jesus' condemnation of divorce while allowing for separation without remarriage.

This latter interpretation finds support in Paul's prohibition against divorce (1 Cor 7:10-11), as well as nearly 2000 years of established tradition in the Catholic church.

The second New Testament text suggesting a less than absolute condemnation of divorce is found in Paul's First Letter to the Corinthians. Here Paul addresses himself to the Christian who is married to an unbeliever. He tells the Christian partner in such a marriage that he or she should remain faithful to the marriage for as long as the unbelieving partner is willing to remain married (1 Cor 7:12-14). But then he adds:

> If the unbeliever wishes to separate, however, let him do so. The believing husband or wife is not bound in such cases.
>
> (1 Cor 7:15)

Saint Paul is not dealing with the "great mystery" of two baptized Christians entering into the indissolvable bond of marrying in the Lord. Rather, he is dealing with the painful situation of a Christian married by civil law to an unbelieving spouse who refuses to remain married. In such cases, Paul says, the Christian is not bound to force the unbelieving partner to continue in a marriage he or she no longer wants.

By the fourth century, the church used this text to conclude that the Christian partner in this situation was never in a valid marriage "in the Lord." Therefore, the Christian could not only separate, but also remarry. This church tradition became known as the *Pauline Privilege.*

As we shall see in a later chapter which deals with annulments, there is a growing number of instances when divorced Catholics have been allowed to remarry in the church. But whenever an annulment occurs it is because there is substantial evidence that the divorced person's first marriage vows were not valid. Church practice today continues to uphold the principle that a valid Christian marriage shares in the indissoluble bond of love between Christ and his body the church, and as such is a union which by its very nature is permanent and indissoluble.

As a class, list on the board and discuss what you think contributes to today's high divorce rate. How could a shared and sincerely lived Christian faith help a couple meet each of these challenges to a lasting marriage?

Marriage and the Second Coming of Christ

The New Testament teachings on marriage were shaped partly by the early church's imminent *eschatology*. In other words, the early church expected Christ's second coming to occur soon (1 Cor 7:29).

The first Christians were convinced that Christ's second coming would occur within their own lifetime. As can be imagined, this expectancy gave a sense of urgency to Christian life, which in turn affected the church's attitudes toward marriage. In this vein, Paul writes to the Corinthians:

> I tell you, brothers, the time is short. From now on those with wives should live as though they had none; those who weep should live as though they were not weeping, and those who rejoice as though they were not rejoicing; buyers should conduct themselves as though they owned nothing, and those who make use of the world as though they were not using it, for the world as we know it is passing away.
>
> (1 Cor 7:29-31)

These themes of the shortness of time and the need to turn from what is passing to what is eternal are uniquely significant to married Christians because their lives are inevitably and deeply involved in the affairs of the world. Making a living, caring for a home, having sexual relations and raising children are all integral to married life. And for this reason married Christians are more vulnerable to the folly of basing their lives upon what is passing away. Within the context of this vulnerability Paul upholds virginity as being a valid Christian response not only to the Gospel, but also to the temporary nature of this world, destined to end with Christ's second coming (1 Cor 7:32-35).

Accompanying this vulnerability, however, is a unique opportunity for the Christian couple to give witness to Christ in the world. By being married in the Lord, the Christian couple can discover Christ hidden in the very center of human experience. Thus, when carried out in a spirit of faith, such activities as making a living, caring for a home, having sexual relations and raising children are not obstacles to the couple's union with Christ. On the contrary, these actions and concerns are the very means through which the couple encounters Christ hidden in their lives.

With this discovery, the Christian husband and wife also discover their calling to reveal Christ's hidden presence by allowing his love to appear in their actions toward one another, their children, and all they meet. This style of living reveals just how intimate and all-embracing Christ's love for us really is. By their shared faith in Christ, they give witness to Christ present in the market-place, the home, and in every instance where our life touches the lives of others.

---

1. Why do you think it is difficult for a Christian married couple to avoid becoming dominated by materialistic values and the pressure to "get ahead in the world"?

2. What are some specific ways a Christian couple could put into action their commitment to love each other, children and others as Christ has loved them?

"Wives Be Submissive to Your Husbands"

As a way of concluding this chapter, we will examine the question of whether or not there is a conflict between the changing role of today's women and certain teachings of the New Testament. For example, Paul's letter to the Ephesians states:

> Wives should be submissive to their husbands as if to the Lord because the husband is head of his wife just as Christ is head of his body the church, as well as its savior.
>
> (Eph 5:22-23)

In order to understand Paul's position regarding women, we must first recall his basic assertion that "there does not exist among you . . . male nor female" (Gal 3:28). In Christ there is a perfect equality between men and women. Besides this equality, Paul also tells Christian husbands that they must love their wives "as Christ loved the church" (Eph 5:25). From this we can conclude that a husband's love, being like Christ's love, is to be devoid of any domineering, insensitive or unfair attitudes and actions. It must be Christ and not the husband that rules over the Christian home.

With this equality and love established, we are still faced with the question of a Christian wife's obedience to her husband. Does the New Testament teach that a wife should submit to her husband's loving authority over her?

In responding to this question, we must remember that a Christian marriage in the infant church was an ordinary, secular marriage which the Christian husband and wife were to experience in the Lord. Thus, in determining norms for a husband-wife relationship, Paul simply adapted the household codes of conduct observed in his day. These codes of conduct assumed that the place of the woman was "at the hearth and the loom." He assumed that it was proper for a woman to accept a social order in which she was not allowed to receive an education, hold a political office or engage in other activities considered proper only for men.

In reading Paul's assertion that women should be subject to their husbands, we must keep in mind that parts of Scripture simply reflect current beliefs and practices. For example, Paul urged his friend Philemon to trust his runaway slave, Onesimus, but in doing so he apparently saw no problem with the institution of slavery. In the Old Testament, Abram had sexual relations with his maid-servant Hagar when his wife, Sarai, was unable to bear children. Rather than revealing God's will for us, Abram's action simply reflects the custom of his time (Gn 16:1-4).

Seen in this way, we can say that a wife's subjection to her husband is no more a matter of Christian doctrine than is Paul's directive that women should keep their heads covered in church (1 Cor 11:5-6). In other words, a wife's subjection to her husband is a matter of culture and personal preference rather than a matter of Christian faith. What *is* a matter of Christian faith is that both husband and wife love one another as Christ has loved his church.

---

1. Would you agree that until very recently our laws and customs have promoted an unfair and authoritarian treatment of women by men?

2. As a class, list on the board what you think are the positive and negative factors in current trends regarding the role of women. After the lists are complete, discuss how Christian values might be related positively or negatively to each of these factors.

SUMMARY

1. Both parenthood and romantic-sexual love are revealed in the Old Testament to contribute to the nature and dignity of marriage.

2. Marriage shares in the natural holiness of God's creation. Consequently, marriages in Old Testament times took place in the home as a family celebration without involvement in the synagogue or temple.

3. Marriage shares in the mystery of evil. Sin and selfishness can dominate the marriage relationship. A couple must work together to direct their marriage toward God.

4. A Christian marriage expresses the "great mystery" of Christ's love for us.

5. Because a Christian marriage participates in our union with Christ, it is by its very nature permanent and indissoluble.

6. Paul's teaching about wives being subject to their husbands is not a matter of Christian revelation, but simply a reflection of the customs and attitudes of Paul's day.

EVALUATION

Using your own words, write an essay summarizing this chapter, using one well-developed paragraph for each of the six points listed above.

RESEARCH PROJECTS

1. Research present-day Jewish wedding practices and report your findings to the class.

2. Review recent articles in Catholic magazines and read one or two recent books on the theme of the church's involve-

ment in and reaction to the changing role of women in both society in general and in the church.

CREATIVE PROJECT

Imagine that your best friend is getting married and you have been asked to give the homily at the wedding. Prepare a homily on marriage by incorporating some of what you learned in this chapter into what you personally think are the most important elements of married love.

4
Marriage in the Tradition of the Church

Let the goods of marriage be loved:
offspring, fidelity, and the sacrament.
—St. Augustine

This chapter will examine the ways in which the church's understanding and celebration of marriage have developed over the nearly 2000 years from the time of Christ to our own day. The chapter is divided into three parts: 1) a look at one or two of the developments in the church's understanding and celebration of marriage that took place during each of the major periods of the church's history; 2) a brief description of the process involved in getting married in the church today; and 3) the marriage liturgy as it is celebrated today.

THE TIME OF THE FATHERS

The Fathers of the church were the great theologians whose writings guided and inspired the early church. They were influential from the first and second centuries, starting with the writings of Saint Ignatius of Antioch and Saint Justin Martyr, to the middle of the eighth century with the writings of Saint John Damascene.

The Beginnings of a Marriage Liturgy

A significant development of this period was the beginning of a marriage liturgy in the form of a blessing said over the couple by the local bishop. Evidence of this blessing is found in the writings of Saint Ignatius of Antioch who wrote to his fellow bishop, Polycarp:

> It is proper to enter into the marriage union with the sanction of the bishop: thus the marriage will be acceptable to the Lord and not just gratify lust.

This blessing by the bishop was not, however, a universal custom at this time. Nor can we assume that the bishop's blessing mentioned by Ignatius was anything close to a marriage liturgy as we know it today. In fact, marriage liturgies for Christians were not obligatory until the 11th century. For quite some time, the church considered the real marriage between Christians to be the civil, secular ceremony which took place in the procession of the bride to the bridegroom's home. At first, the bishop's blessing was little more than a blessing upon the couple's union and a reminder to them that they were to experience their marriage in the Lord.

By the reign of Pope Damasus in the fourth century, however, we find evidence in Rome that this blessing of the bishop gradually evolved into a true liturgical celebration in which the priest or bishop placed a veil on the bride. With this veiling of the bride, it was said that "the marriage was celebrated by God, himself, in heaven." By the fifth-century reign of Pope Sixtus III, there was a Nuptial Mass and also a more fully developed ritual surrounding the church's blessing upon the couple married in the church. In short, during this early period there was a growing awareness in the church that the faith dimension of married love between Christians should be celebrated and expressed in the liturgical prayers of the believing community centered around the local bishop or priest. However, it would be quite some time before this awareness became expressed in the form of universal church practice.

Make a list of three important events and the ritual celebrations or customs that express their importance. Your list should consist of one event and ritual celebration or custom from each of the following areas: 1) personal life; 2) history of our country, and 3) the life of Christ.

Event	Celebration or custom
personal _____	_____
_____	_____
national _____	_____
_____	_____
Christian _____	_____
_____	_____

After sharing your answers as a class, discuss why you think we use ritual celebrations to express our involvement in the important events of our lives. What does the early church's growing awareness of the need to ritualize and celebrate the faith dimension of marriage suggest about the church's awareness of the importance of marriage in Christian life?

Saint Augustine: The Three Goods of Marriage

A second contribution during this period of the church's history was made by Saint Augustine, the great Father of the church and bishop of North Africa. His contribution to the church's understanding of marriage can be summarized in his statement, "Let the goods of marriage be loved: offspring, fidelity, and the sacrament." By combining these three elements found in Scripture, Augustine provided the basis of much of the church's subsequent reflection on marriage.

Offspring: Mentioning children as a good of marriage may seem unnecessary in that most people readily assume that children and family life play a vital role in married life. Yet in Augustine's day, some members of a group called the Manichaeans taught that marriage and having children were evil. In our own society, the media often portray marriages that place the pursuit of pleasure and possessions over children and family life.

Augustine refers to the Book of Genesis which recounts God's creation of man and woman and his command to increase and multiply. Through this and other passages Augustine affirms the scriptural teaching that children are a blessing from God and an essential element of married life.

Fidelity: Marital fidelity is directly linked to having and raising children, since children need a loving and stable environment in which to grow and develop. Augustine teaches the scriptural ideal that marital fidelity is a living expression of God's fidelity to his people. God will never cease to love and care for us, a husband and wife should never cease to love and care for one another.

The Sacrament: There are two distinct and important themes underlying Augustine's understanding of the term "sacrament." The first theme is that a sacrament is a *sacred sign* which expresses and shares in the mystery of our union with God in Christ. Thus, following Paul's letter to the Ephesians (5:32), Augustine sees the marriage between two baptized Christians as being a sacred sign of the "great mystery" of our share in Christ's never-ending love for us.

The second theme in Augustine's notion of sacrament is taken from the classical Latin word *sacramentum,* meaning a sacred commitment or oath to which one was legally bound. Augustine combined the two themes, sacred sign and binding commitment, to hold that marriage is a binding, indissoluble commitment precisely because it is a sacred, living sign of our indissoluble union with God in Christ.

The exercise below is intended to foster an appreciation for Augustine's notion of the threefold dignity of marriage.

A. Gather into small groups. Each group is to select one of the five aspects of fidelity given in the list below and write the underlined word indicating its choice in the circle marked "A."

1. Faithfully *supporting* and complementing one's spouse, stressing strengths instead of weaknesses.

2. Fidelity in being *open* and honest, so your spouse knows your true thoughts and feelings.

3. Fidelity in being *sensitive* enough to notice the little things that are part of the "ups and downs" of daily life.

4. Faithfully *forgiving* one's spouse when he or she has done wrong.

5. Fidelity in being *trustworthy* and trusting, that is, letting your spouse know he or she can rely on you to be faithful, and that you know you can trust him or her to do the same.

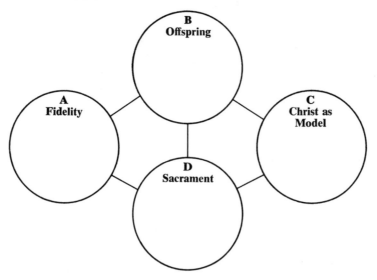

B. Next, in circle B of the diagram, write a sentence stating why the aspect of fidelity your group has chosen is also very important in the relationship between parents and either small or teenage children.

C. Third, either from memory or by looking through the Gospels, find an action or saying of Jesus illustrating how he embodied within himself the aspect of fidelity the group has chosen. Write a brief sentence describing the action or saying of Jesus in circle C.

D. Finally, for circle D, each member of the group should compose a paragraph stating how a couple who model their love for one another and their children on Christ can be said to be a *living sign* of Christ's presence in the world.

THE MIDDLE AGES

The Middle Ages span from about the end of the fifth century (the fall of the Roman Empire) to about the mid-14th century (the beginning of the Italian Renaissance). Two major developments in the church's understanding and celebration of marriage which occurred during this period are: 1) the formation of a completely church-centered marriage, and 2) the formal recognition of marriage as one of the seven sacraments.

A Church-Centered Marriage

The medieval transition of marriage from the home to the church was both gradual and complex. Certainly one important factor in this change involved the church's moral responsibility to speak out against abuses of the day regarding marriage. For example, church authorities were obligated to oppose the custom of a king giving a girl in marriage to a man after that girl had already been betrothed to someone else. Similarly, the church opposed incestuous marriages and the custom among the converted Germanic tribes of abducting a woman and forcing her into marriage. The church's condemnation of these and other practices was expressed in the form of lists of *impediments* to marriage, that is, of obstacles to the Christian dignity of marriage.

One set of abuses involved clandestine marriages, or marriages conducted in secret between the spouses without any witnesses. Interestingly enough the church still considered such marriages valid as long as both spouses gave their free consent to the marriage. But, as in the case of the Germanic tribes where a man could carry a woman off physically and claim her for his wife, these secret marriages became occasions for women being forced to marry. They also became occasions for homes to be broken up, as one or both of the spouses might later claim that they had made no secret marriage vows.

In response to these abuses, the bishops of the Synod of Lyons held in 541 urged that all marriage between Christians be public, have parental permission and the customary ceremonial practices.

This movement toward public marriage took place at a time when the church was becoming the focal point of the political, economic and judicial structures of medieval society. In effect the church and state became one. Not only was the cathedral the architectural center of the town, but more significantly, the church was the center of people's lives. Citizenship was built upon membership in the church.

The trend toward church marriage did not take place overnight. In fact, as late as the middle of the ninth century, Pope Nicholas I stated that no sin was involved if a Christian couple chose to be married with no liturgical prayers or blessings by the priest, as long as both spouses gave their free consent.

Despite this very gradual development, a totally church-centered marriage eventually became the universal practice of the church. Certainly by the 11th and 12th centuries the civil laws and customs regarding marriage had become totally absorbed into the laws and rituals of the church. The church came to speak of marriage in the legal terms of a binding contract, the validity of which was determined by church authority. Church authority made it a matter of church law that all marriages between Christians be celebrated by a marriage liturgy conducted by a priest. In his role as representative of the church, the priest became the central witness of the Christian marriage.

As mentioned above, the medieval church recognized *impediments* to a Christian marriage. The questions below are taken from a typical prenuptial investigation form used by the church today in questioning engaged couples seeking marriage in the church.

As a class, discuss why each impediment remains a major obstacle to marriage in the church:

1. Are you related by blood, marriage or in any other way to your intended spouse?

2. Have you ever been married, or attempted marriage, or lived in common-law relationship with anyone?

3. Have you ever made a vow that is inconsistent with the married state?

4. Do you intend to enter a permanent marriage lasting until death?

5. Do you intend to be faithful to each other for life?

6. Is there any person or circumstances forcing you to enter this marriage against your will?

Marriage as a Sacrament

The process of bringing the marriage ceremony from the home to the church accompanied the church's growing awareness of Christian marriage as one of the seven sacraments. The word "sacrament" is derived from the Latin word *sacramentum,* which in turn is derived from the Greek word *mysterion,* which Saint Paul used to describe the mystery of our union with God through Christ. Taken in its most basic Christian sense, the term "sacrament" can then be said to refer to Christ as the Perfect Sacrament of God's love and mercy in our lives.

It is within this context that Augustine referred to marriage as a sacrament. In doing so, he meant that through faith in Christ, a Christian couple could experience the presence and love of Christ in each other. Because Christ's love united them in the Lord, their union is itself a sacrament of Christ's love.

When Peter Lombard, a 12th-century bishop of Paris, described marriage as a sacrament of the church, he was making a formal statement of what the church had come to recognize as the significance of marriage: that is, married love between Christians is a living sign, an encounter with and expression of the undying love of Christ for us.

In another sense, the marriage liturgy is a celebration and beginning of a lifelong sacrament of the couple's life together. In this sense the marriage liturgy is a celebration of the holiness of life itself as redeemed by Christ. In it the couple expresses their faith. As they live each day, as they talk, embrace, laugh or experience hardship, they are in the presence of Christ.

THE COUNCIL OF TRENT

The Council of Trent marked a new phase in the church's history. When the bishops gathered in Council in December 1545, their purpose was twofold: 1) to correct abuses within the church; and 2) to strengthen the church in the painful and confusing aftermath of the Protestant Reformation.

Martin Luther and the other Protestant reformers agreed with Rome that the church had the right and obligation to offer counsel and guidance in helping Christians determine whom and under what conditions they might choose to marry. The Protestants, however, denied that the church had any judicial authority to list impediments to marriage. The Protestant Christians, in other words, denied that the church had a right to move from giving advice and counsel to exercising legal authority over Christians seeking to get married in the church.

In reaffirming the church's position on this matter, the bishops of the Council of Trent stated that the pope and bishops of the Roman Catholic Church had received from Christ authority over the sacraments and all matters of faith and morals (Mt 16:13-19). In response to the reformers' objections, the bishops stated that the problem was not judicial authority but the uneven application of that authority throughout the world. Hence, one of the results of the Council of Trent was the emergence of universal church laws governing marriage.

THE CHURCH TODAY

Except for a few minor revisions, the practices and attitudes dictated by the Council of Trent remained virtually unchanged until the Second Vatican Council (1962-66) when Pope John XXIII called the bishops to council to face the complex and challenging problem of adjusting the church of the Council of Trent to the needs of the Christians living in today's rapidly changing world.

With respect to marriage in particular, the bishops at the Council both affirmed the biblical and traditional values of Christian marriage and cautioned against the threats to those values. In affirming the value of Christian marriage, the bishops stated:

> Christ the Lord abundantly blesses this many-faceted love (of marriage) welling up as it does from the fountain of divine love and structured as it is on the model of his union with his church. For as God of old made himself present to his people through a covenant of love and fidelity, so now the Savior of men and the Spouse of the church comes into the lives of married Christians through the sacrament of matrimony.

(The Church in the Modern World, no. 47)

And, in cautioning Christians against the trends and attitudes opposed to the values of Christian marriage, the bishops said:

> The excellence of this institution (of marriage) is not everywhere reflected with equal brilliance, since polygamy, the plague of divorce, so-called free love and other disfigurements have an obscuring effect. In addition, married love is too often profaned by excessive self-love, the worship of pleasure and illicit practices against human generation. Moreover, serious disturbances are caused in families by modern economic conditions, by influences at once social and psychological, and by the demands of civil society. Finally, in certain parts of the world problems resulting from population growth are generating concern.

(The Church in the Modern World, no. 47)

The bishops at the Second Vatican Council did much more than simply affirm the holiness of marriage and caution against the forces in contemporary society that threaten the dignity of marriage. The bishops also helped married Christians realize their responsibility to play a more active and central role in the life of the church. The bishops did this less by what they said about marriage than by what they said about the place of the laity, most of whom are married, in the church.

The bishops proclaimed the church to be the people of God, a community of men and women in which lay people, clergy and religious are called to *one,* single perfection as disciples of Christ:

> Fortified by so many and such powerful means of salvation, *all* the faithful, whatever their condition or state, are called by the Lord, each in his own way, to that holy perfection whereby the Father himself is perfect.
>
> *(Constitution on the Church,* no. 11)

Since a majority of lay Christians live out their lives as married couples, the bishops stressed the vital role that married Christians should play by actively witnessing to Christ's love both in the home and in the daily affairs of the secular world. In short, the bishops' contribution to Christian marriage was that of helping married Christians realize their full dignity as members of the people of God:

> The family was established by God as the vital and fundamental cell of society. To fulfill its divine purpose, it should, by the mutual devotion of its members and by their prayer made in common to God, become, as it were, a domestic extension of the church's sanctuary; the whole family should involve itself in the liturgical worship of the church; finally, the family should show itself hospitable, just and generous of its resources in the service of all its brothers who are in need.
>
> *(Decree on the Apostolate of the Laity,* no. 11)

Select members of the class to go, possibly in small groups if they are from the same parish, and interview the pastor or assistant about the following programs by which married couples can participate in parish life.

1. *Parish Council* in which the lay people of the parish *share* responsibility for the growth and development of parish life.

2. *Baptismal, First Communion and Confirmation programs* which involve some kind of active participation of the parents in their children's spiritual growth.

3. *Adult education and family-centered education programs* geared to the need of married and young adult Christians living in today's world.

4. *Lay liturgical ministers' program* in which lay people serve as lectors, commentators and ministers of the Eucharist.

5. *Social action groups* which serve the needs of the poor, the elderly, the ill and others who are in special need.

6. *Youth groups* that provide both recreation and a sense of community for the teenagers in the parish.

Report the findings to the class. How does participation in these activities support marriage and family life? Is it possible that these activities might interfere with family life? Discuss what else might be done in a parish to help married Christians live more committed Christian lives.

A Current Concern

Many Catholic couples are concerned about the present high divorce rate and, in particular, about the increase of divorce among Catholics. Especially disturbing to some is the number of Catholics who apparently remarry in the church.

This new trend does not represent any departure from the church's fidelity to Christ's teachings about the permanence of marriage. The church continues to hold that a valid Christian marriage is indissoluble. However, for serious reasons and as a last resort, a validly married Christian couple may separate. But they still remain married and are not free to remarry someone else.

The church, however, is changing its attitudes toward Catholics who have gotten a separation and a civil divorce. Formerly, divorced Catholics were all but ignored by the church and even mistakenly considered "excommunicated." Little if anything was done to acknowledge their presence or to serve their spiritual, social or emotional needs. Today, many dioceses have programs to help Catholics recover from the trauma of a divorce. Many parishes hold regular meetings in which divorced Catholics, usually under the trained leadership of a priest, can draw strength and encouragement from one another as they learn to build a new life.

With regard to remarriage, the church is attempting to develop a more refined understanding of the requirements for a valid, hence indissoluble, Christian marriage. In other words, the church is attempting to determine with greater accuracy those situations in which a valid Christian marriage did not exist because the requirements for such a marriage were not fulfilled. In cases where it can be determined that valid sacramental marriage did not exist, the church can issue a formal statement called an *annulment,* leaving the Catholic free to remarry in the church if he or she so chooses.

To enter into a valid Christian marriage, a couple must: 1) have a sincere desire to live a Christian life; 2) enter into the marriage freely and with full knowledge of the seriousness of the commitment; 3) be capable of actually carrying out the church's vision of married life; 4) be open to having children of their own; 5) have no previous vow or valid marriage; and 6) be married in the presence of a priest or minister, who represents Christ present in the believing community, and two witnesses.

When these requirements are met, the couple's marriage is valid in the eyes of the church. No annulment is possible. However, when it can be proved that one or more of the above requirements were not fulfilled, then an annulment may be granted. Examples of situations in which an annulment may be granted are: 1) the couple marrying *only* because they "had to," *only* because the girl was pregnant (lack of free will); 2) the couple getting married when grossly immature (lack of full knowledge); 3) the husband or wife being a serious and chronic alcoholic at the time of the wedding (unable to carry out the duties of a loving spouse and parent).

Formerly all applications for annulment were sent to Rome, sometimes taking years to resolve. At this time, however, under an experimental program, most marriage cases are handled by the tribunal office of each diocese, a quicker and more efficient process. In all cases the church is bound to be faithful to both the teachings of Christ on the indissolubility of marriage and the pastoral needs of the Catholic Christian caught in the midst of a regrettable, painful and complex crossroads of life.

Growing sensitivity to the problems of married couples has also resulted in an increase in good pre-marriage programs for engaged couples. With such programs an engaged couple has a better opportunity to understand the unique and serious nature of what it means to be married in the church.

Gather into small groups. Compile a list of five of the most painful aspects of going through a divorce. After all the groups are finished, compare and discuss the lists. What are the spiritual, psychological and social needs of the divorced?

Getting Married in the Church

We now turn to a brief description of some of the practical details involved in getting married in the church today. Of course specific details vary from one diocese or parish to the next. But in general what follows describes the process of an engaged couple preparing for their marriage in the church.

The engaged couple usually begin their marriage plans with a visit to the parish rectory. Many parishes require that a couple come to the rectory at least three times prior to the wedding. The primary purpose of the first visit is to have an honest and open discussion about the presence of faith in the couple's relationship. It is also at this time that they become acquainted with the priest or deacon who will be the celebrant of their marriage liturgy, and reserve the church for their wedding. Most parishes require that the couple reserve the church at least three months prior to the wedding.

On the second visit to the rectory, the future bride and groom respond separately to the questions asked on a prenuptial investigation form. The purpose of these questions is primarily to make sure there are no impediments to a valid marriage in the church. For example, the prenuptial investigation form verifies that one or both of the spouses are not already married and that neither is being forced into the marriage. These and similar questions provide another opportunity to discuss the values of a marriage based upon Christian faith.

The third visit is used to plan the marriage liturgy. Since the Second Vatican Council, great strides have been taken in allowing the couple to select the readings, music and other details that make their wedding more personal.

Along with the sessions in the rectory, the couple also may be required to take part in some form of premarital instructions. In the past, and still in some areas, these instructions have taken the form of Pre-Cana Conferences in which a number of engaged couples attend a series of conferences covering different aspects of married life.

More recently a number of dioceses have been turning from the Pre-Cana Conferences to living room dialogue programs. In such programs the engaged couple goes to the home of a married couple in the parish. The married couple share with the engaged couple their own experiences of married life. Often this sharing allows the engaged couple to express their own concerns and hopes for their future life together.

As a final and practical preparation, there is usually a full wedding rehearsal on the night before the wedding. This is to make sure that the ceremony will go smoothly. All the members of the wedding party are included in the rehearsal to give them a clear understanding of their parts in the ceremony. All of these activities, from the first visit to the rectory to the wedding rehearsal, have but one basic purpose: to help the couple enter into marriage in a mature, enlightened manner that is sensitive to the Christian faith dimensions of married love.

In the case of an interfaith marriage, the couple goes through the same process described above. However, because one person is not Catholic, the couple may be asked to attend a short series of instructions about Catholic beliefs and practices. These instructions are not intended to convert the non-Catholic partner. Rather, they serve to inform the non-Catholic about the faith life of his or her future spouse. Very often these open, adult sharing sessions are beneficial to the Catholic party as well.

The Marriage Liturgy

The marriage liturgy with the options for scripture readings is given below. Going through it as a class will give a clearer picture of the faith dimension of marriage that the wedding ceremony expresses. The "Rite for the Celebration of Marriage Outside Mass" is used here because it can more easily be used in the classroom setting.

Decide if you want to have a mock wedding in class complete with wedding gown, best man, maid of honor, a reception and all the other details of a real wedding. Besides being a lot of fun, such an activity can provide a valuable learning experience of the marriage liturgy and all that goes into the planning of a wedding.

RITE FOR CELEBRATING MARRIAGE OUTSIDE MASS

Entrance Rite and Liturgy of the Word

39. *At the appointed time, the priest, wearing surplice and white stole (or a white cope, if desired), proceeds with the ministers to the door of the church or, if more suitable, to the altar. There he greets the bride and bridegroom in a friendly manner, showing that the church shares their joy.*

   Where it is desirable that the rite of welcome be omitted, the celebration of matrimony begins at once with the liturgy of the word.

40. *If there is a procession to the altar, the ministers go first, followed by the priest, and then the bride and bridegroom. According to local custom, they may be escorted by at least their parents and the two witnesses. Meanwhile, the entrance song is sung.*

   Then the people are greeted, and the prayer is offered, unless a brief pastoral exhortation seems more desirable.

41. *The liturgy of the word takes place in the usual manner. There may be three readings, the first of them from the Old Testament.*

42. *After the Gospel, the priest gives a homily drawn from the sacred text. He speaks about the mystery of Christian marriage, the dignity of wedded love, the grace of the sacrament, and the responsibilities of married people, keeping in mind the circumstances of this particular marriage.*

Rite of Marriage

43. *All stand, including the bride and bridegroom, and the priest addresses them in these or similar words:*

   My dear friends, you have come together in this church so that the Lord may seal and strengthen your love in the presence of the church's minister and this community. Christ abundantly blesses this love. He has already consecrated you in baptism and now he enriches and strengthens you by a special sacrament so that you may assume the duties of marriage in mutual and lasting fidelity. And so, in the presence of the church, I ask you to state your intentions.

44. *The priest then questions them about their freedom of choice, faithfulness to each other, and the acceptance and upbringing of children:*

N. and N., have you come here freely and without reservation to give yourselves to each other in marriage?

Will you love and honor each other as man and wife for the rest of your lives?

The following question may be omitted if, for example, the couple is advanced in years.

Will you accept children lovingly from God, and bring them up according to the law of Christ and his church?

Each answers the questions separately.

Consent

45. *The priest invites them to declare their consent:*

Since it is your intention to enter into marriage, join your right hands, and declare your consent before God and his church.

They join hands.
The bridegroom says:

I, N., take you, N., to be my wife. I promise to be true to you in good times and in bad, in sickness and in health. I will love you and honor you all the days of my life.

The bride says:

I, N., take you, N., to be my husband. I promise to be true to you in good times and in bad, in sickness and in health. I will love you and honor you all the days of my life.

If, however, it seems preferable for pastoral reasons, the priest may obtain consent from the couple through questions. First he asks the bridegroom:

N., do you take N. to be your wife? Do you promise to be true to her in good times and in bad, in sickness and in health, to love her and honor her all the days of your life?

The bridegroom: I do.

Then he asks the bride:

N., do you take N. to be your husband? Do you promise to be true to him in good times and in bad, in sickness and in health, to love him and honor him all the days of your life?

The bride: I do.

In the dioceses of the United States, the following alternative form may be used:

I, N., take you, N., for my lawful wife (husband), to have and to hold, from this day forward, for better, for worse, for richer, for poorer, in sickness and in health, until death do us part.

If it seems preferable for pastoral reasons for the priest to obtain consent from the couple through questions, in the dioceses of the United States the following alternative form may be used:

N., do you take N. for your lawful wife (husband), to have and to hold, from this day forward, for better, for worse, for richer, for poorer, in sickness and in health, until death do you part?

I do.

If pastoral necessity demands it, the conference of bishops may decree that the priest should always obtain the consent of the couple through questions.

46.   *Receiving their consent, the priest says:*

You have declared your consent before the church. May the Lord in his goodness strengthen your consent and fill you both with his blessings.

What God has joined, men must not divide.

R.   Amen.

Blessing and Exchange of Rings

47   *Priest:*

May the Lord bless + these rings which you give to each other as the sign of your love and fidelity.

R.   Amen.

48. *The bridegroom places his wife's ring on her ring finger. He may say:*

N., take this ring as a sign of my love and fidelity. In the name of the Father, and of the Son, and of the Holy Spirit.

The bride places her husband's ring on his ring finger. She may say:

N., take this ring as a sign of my love and fidelity. In the name of the Father, and of the Son, and of the Holy Spirit.

General Intercessions and Nuptial Blessings

49. *The general intercessions (prayer of the faithful) and the blessing of the couple take place in this order:*

(a) *First the priest uses the invitatory of any blessing of the couple or any other, taken from the approved formulas for the general intercessions.*

(b) *Immediately after the invitatory, there can be either a brief silence, or a series of petitions from the prayer of the faithful with responses by the people. All the petitions should be in harmony with the blessing which follows, but should not duplicate it.*

(c) *Then, omitting the prayer that concludes the prayer of the faithful, the priest extends his hands and blesses the bride and bridegroom.*

50. *This blessing may be "Father, by your power" or another.*

> Father, by your power you have made everything out of nothing.
> In the beginning you created the universe
> and made mankind in your own likeness.
> You gave man the constant help of woman
> so that man and woman should no longer be two, but one flesh,
> and you teach us that what you have united
> may never be divided.
>
> Father, you have made the union of man and wife so holy a mystery

that it symbolizes the marriage of Christ and his church.

Father, by your plan man and woman are united,
and married life has been established
as the one blessing that was not forfeited by original sin
or washed away in the flood.

Look with love upon this woman, your daughter,
now joined to her husband in marriage.
She asks your blessing.
Give her the grace of love and peace.
May she always follow the example of the holy women
whose praises are sung in the scriptures.

May her husband put his trust in her
and recognize that she is his equal
and the heir with him to the life of grace.
May he always honor her and love her
as Christ loves his bride, the church.

Father, keep them always true to your commandments.
Keep them faithful in marriage
and let them be living examples of Christian life.

Give them the strength which comes from the Gospel
so that they may be witnesses of Christ to others.
(Bless them with children
and help them to be good parents.
May they live to see their children's children.)
And, after a happy old age,
grant them fullness of life with the saints
in the kingdom of heaven.

Conclusion of the Celebration

51. *The entire rite can be concluded with the Lord's Prayer and
the blessing*

And may almighty God bless you all,
the Father, and the Son, + and the Holy Spirit.

or with another form.

SCRIPTURE TEXTS TO BE USED IN THE MARRIAGE RITE

**Old Testament
Readings**

**New Testament
Readings**

Genesis 1:26-28, 31a

Genesis 2:18-24

*Genesis 24:48-51,
58-67*

*Tobit 7:9c-10,
11c-17 (Vulgate)*

Tobit 8:5-10

*Song of Songs
2:8-10, 14, 16a;
8:6-7a*

*Ecclesiasticus
26:1-4, 16-21
(Greek 1-4, 13-16)*

*Jeremiah 31:31-32a,
33-34a*

*Romans 8:31b-35,
37-39*

*Romans 12:1-2,
9-18 (longer) or 1-2,
9-13 (shorter)*

*I Corinthians 6:13c-
15a, 17-20*

*I Corinthians 12:31-
13:8a*

*Ephesians 5:2a,
21-33 (longer) or
2a, 25-32 (shorter)*

Colossians 3:12-17

I Peter 3:19

I John 3:18-24

I John 4:7-12

*Revelation 19:1,
5-9a*

Responsorial Psalms

Psalm 33:12 and 18, 20-21, 22
R.   (5b)   The earth is full of the goodness
of the Lord.

Psalm 34:2-3, 4-5, 6-7, 8-9
R.   (2a)   I will bless the Lord at all times.
OR: (9a)   Taste and see the goodness of
the Lord.

Psalm 103:1-2, 8 and 13, 17-18a

R.   (8a)   The Lord is kind and merciful.
OR: (17)   The Lord's kindness is ever-
lasting to those who fear him.

Psalm 112:1-2, 3-4, 5-7a, 7bc-8, 9
R.   (1b)   Happy are those who do what the
Lord commands.
OR: Alleluia.

Psalm 128:1-2, 3, 4-5
R.   (1a)   Happy are those who fear the
Lord.
OR: (4)   See how the Lord blesses those
who fear him.

Psalm 145:8-9, 10 and 15, 17-18
R.   (9a)   The Lord is compassionate to all
his creatures.

Psalm 148:1-2, 3-4, 9-10, 11-12ab, 12c-14a
R.   (12c)   Let all praise the name of the
Lord.
OR: Alleluia.

Alleluia Verse and Verse Before the Gospel

I John 4:8 and 11

I John 4:12

I John 4:16

I John 4:7b

Gospel Readings

Matthew 5:1-12

Matthew 5:13-16

Matthew 7:21,
24-29 (longer) 21,
24-25 (shorter)

Matthew 19:3-6

Matthew 22:35-40

Mark 10:6-9

John 2:1-11

John 15:9-12

John 15:12-16

John 17:20-26
(longer) 20-23
(shorter)

SUMMARY

1. The church's present way of understanding and celebrating marriage is the result of nearly 2000 years of development.

2. In the time of the Fathers, the church began the first stages of a marriage liturgy. Saint Augustine wrote about marriage in terms of offspring, fidelity and sacrament.

3. In the Middle Ages Christian marriage became wholly absorbed into the rituals and laws of the church. The church formally recognized marriage as one of the seven sacraments.

4. With the Council of Trent the church made marriage laws and customs of marriage uniform throughout the world.

5. After the Second Vatican Council there has been a greater sense of awareness and concern for the needs of married Christians.

EVALUATION

Write one well-developed paragraph for each of the historical developments of the church's understanding of marriage that have been presented in this chapter.

GUEST SPEAKERS

Invite Protestant ministers to speak to the class about their denominations' understanding of Christian marriage and how it is celebrated.

SCRIPTURE EXERCISE

Assign small groups the task of looking up and commenting upon a number of the scripture texts used in the marriage liturgy. The commentary, either oral or written, should explain what aspect of married love is reflected upon in each passage.

5

Some Practical Concerns of Married Couples

Wherever you go I will go, wherever you lodge I will lodge, your people shall be my people, and your God my God.
— Ruth

Our final chapter on marriage will examine some practical, everyday concerns of married couples. The chapter will conclude with a reflection on communication and Christian faith as two means of fostering a lasting, happy marriage.

The Question of Compatibility

All married couples, regardless of how strong their love, eventually experience incompatibilities, that is, differences in the way they act, think or feel. Sometimes these differences become so overwhelming that they threaten the marriage itself. In fact, incompatibility due to irreconcilable differences is one of the most frequently cited causes of divorce.

Imagine that each of the couples listed below is very much in love and wants to get married. On a scale of 1 to 5 (with 1 representing the least, and 5 the most) indicate the degree to which you personally think the difference in question will prove to be a major obstacle to the couple forming a lasting relationship. Along with your response, offer a specific situation that might arise which illustrates why you think the way you do.

Bob is white. Lisa is black.

1　2　3　4　5

_____

_____

Bill comes from a devout
Catholic family. He wants
his children to be raised
Catholic. Laura comes
from a devout Baptist
family. She wants her children to be raised Baptist.

1　2　3　4　5

_____

_____

Julie is finishing medical
school. She plans to be-
come a surgeon. Kevin
graduated from high
school. He runs a local gas
station.

1　2　3　4　5

_____

_____

Sue comes from a wealthy
family. Curt's family is
very poor. They plan to
live on Curt's salary as a
high school teacher.

1　2　3　4　5

_____

_____

Angie is 18 years old. Devin
is 35 years old.

1　2　3　4　5

_____

_____

John is anxious to have a
large family. Debbie wants
no children for at least 10
years.

1　2　3　4　5

_____

_____

How important is compromise in areas of incompatibility?
Are there some situations in which compromise would be
wrong because it would mean being untrue to basic principles and beliefs? Does this suggest that sometimes a
couple should not marry even though they are in love?
Explain your answers.

Marital incompatibility is, of course, not restricted to the obvious and dramatic differences indicated in the above exercise. Two
people of relatively equal social and economic background can find
themselves in an apparently irreconcilable conflict. Differences in
personality, sexual and emotional needs, or attitudes about raising
children are but a few of the areas of potential conflict which can
threaten a happy marriage.

In a way incompatibility seems like a surprising and unexpected phenomenon. How can two people who love each other enough to marry find themselves in such disharmony? In instances of divorce or separation due to irreconcilable differences, how can the differences between a husband and wife become stronger than the love that first drew them together?

An insight into the nature of incompatibility is provided by Arthur Ford and Robert L. Zorn in their book, *Why Marriage?* (Argus Communications, 1974). The authors distinguish between "speed" and "depth" in a marriage relationship. "Speed" refers to the strong emotional and physical attraction that first moves a man and woman to seek ever greater degrees of intimacy with one another. As this speed builds, so too do the excitement, anticipation and longing for yet further degrees of intimacy and mutual self-revelation. By its very nature, speed is short-lived.

The term "depth" refers to the mature, free and, at times, difficult task of learning to share one's life with another. Unlike speed, depth is not sudden and automatic. On the contrary, depth must be deliberately and mutually cultivated over a lifetime of fidelity to the demands of love.

As long as the speed of the relationship is maintained, the differences between the couple remain blurred. Like objects viewed fleetingly from the window of a speeding car, potential points of conflict are not brought into focus. However, as the speed of the relationship decreases, the heat of passion is often replaced by the heat of conflict. Without depth, these differences can cause a marriage to die a slow death through misunderstanding and emotional withdrawal.

The question seems to be how to maintain a sense of passion and romance while at the same time achieving the depth that will support the couple in their differences. Of course, there is no single correct way to achieve this goal. Each couple is unique in the way it works at achieving a happy marriage. We can, however, suggest a few considerations about this question of marital compatibility:

- Depth implies a depth of communication. Before getting married, a couple owe it to themselves to take time to communicate honestly and openly about themselves and their future. The notion that marriage automatically solves problems is utterly false. Love must be based upon mature communication if it is to reach a depth that will support a lifetime commitment to marriage. Of course, the need for communication continues after the marriage ceremony. Differences tend *not* to become irreconcilable when both spouses are able to communicate their inner needs and feelings to one another.

- It is true that a married couple must have some shared values and experiences. Two people who are totally different are likely to have an unsuccessful marriage. And yet it is important to keep in mind that mature love seeks *unity* not uniformity. That is, mature love seeks intimacy and union with the partner, not a partner who is identical with the self. What husband or wife would want a spouse who was nothing more than a shadow or clone of himself or herself? A great deal of the fun, adventure and fulfillment of marriage is derived from two people communicating with, respecting and cherishing each other in a love that embraces and unites them in their differences.

- Finally, it is helpful to avoid unrealistic expectations of compatibility in marriage. The perfectly compatible couple does not exist. In fact, we are not even compatible with ourselves. At times, every one of us experiences an inner conflict between our ideals and our actions, our dreams and our abilities. It is inevitable, therefore, that two people, each with his or her own inner incompatibilities, will experience incompatibilities with one another. Again, the depth is the factor which allows them to turn their incompatibilities into occasions for deepening their patience, respect and love for each other.

Money Is Not Everything

A couple deeply in love and thinking of getting married might conceivably be inclined to have little regard for money and its place in their future. But once married life begins, the importance of mature, responsible attitudes toward money becomes very obvious. It is true that money does not buy happiness. But it does buy the shelter, food and other necessities which the couple and their future children need for living. In this regard, an appreciation of and respect for the importance of financial security in marriage can be seen as an important dimension of the mature, responsible love proper to marriage.

Working and planning together to build a sound financial future are important ways by which a couple can express their hopes for the future. Supporting one another in times of financial hardship can bring a couple closer together, and common financial goals are an important expression of a couple's shared values. Whether money is spent to send the children to Catholic schools, to help support aging parents or to go away for a special family vacation, all reflect values that the couple hold in common.

Understandably then, conflicting attitudes and values are often expressed in arguments over money. A couple may argue over whether or not the wife should accept a job at which she will be making more money than her husband. Or a couple may disagree over who should control the family finances. It is not money as such that is the cause of conflict, but rather the couple's conflicting values or expectations.

This is not to say that money cannot be a problem in a marriage. The sustained tension and frayed nerves resulting from a chronic shortage of money can easily spill over into domestic arguments, alcoholism and other problems.

Once again, communication and mature love can be crucial in a couple's handling of money-related problems. By communicating their values and attitudes about money both before and after marriage, financial concerns can be a source of shared responsibility and concern. Mature love can enable a couple to avoid becoming too materialistic in times of financial success. It can also keep the couple from becoming discouraged in times of financial hardship.

A Family Budget:

1. Select volunteer "couples" to put together sample budgets for newlyweds. Remember that a budget reflects a couple's values and priorities as well as how much money they have available to them. Check with a loan officer at a bank, parents or other sources to be sure the figures are realistic for the geographical area in which you live.

Compare and discuss the completed budgets as a class.

How might the budget of a couple trying to live out their Christian commitment differ from the "average" budget for newlyweds in your area?

Expenses	Monthly average
withholding expenses (taxes, FICA, pension, etc.)	_____
rent or house payments	_____
food	_____
utilities	_____
transportation (gas, car payments and maintenance)	_____
insurance (medical, car, life, health, house)	_____
clothes	_____
household needs (cleaning supplies, maintenance)	_____
recreation	
savings	_____
contributions	_____
other	_____

Total monthly expenses _____

Total expenses for the year _____

2. Other "couples" can look into average salaries for various lines of work. For example, what is the average beginning income for an accountant, truck driver, dentist, lawyer, schoolteacher, mechanic, nurse, secretary? Is there a difference in average salary for those who go to college and those who do not? What differences are there in one-income families and two-income families?

3. A third group of "couples" can research the cost of having a baby. Be sure to include the following costs: obstetrician, pediatrician, baby furniture, food, and

clothing. Compute these costs for the first year of the baby's life after birth. Keep in mind the following: the wife may not work after the baby is born.

4. Finally, a fourth group of "couples" look into the price of buying a home. Find the answers to the following: What is the price range of homes in the geographical area where you live? What down payment is required? What are the monthly payments? property tax? home maintenance costs? What income is needed to meet these expenses?

After all the groups have finished their projects, share the findings with the class. Discuss the overall financial picture for a young couple today.

Discuss the following:

a. What are some ways in which married couples can place too much emphasis on material luxuries and the place of money in marriage?

b. When financial problems reach a point where a family is living in poverty, what tensions are likely to occur?

c. It has been said that if a couple is so poor that the man cannot afford to buy an engagement ring, it is a sign that the couple is not yet financially ready for marriage. Do you agree? Do you think that, ideally speaking, a man should graduate from college or finish his job training before he gets married? Should a woman?

On Becoming Parents

Of course, children have a profound effect upon a married couple's relationship. Each stage of a child's life brings new responsibilities as well as new joys into the parents' lives.

Gather into small groups to discuss the burdens and rewards that each phase of a child's development brings to a marriage. Where appropriate, indicate where these burdens and rewards differ with respect to the husband and wife.

	Burdens	**Rewards**
pregnancy	_____	_____
infancy	_____	_____
grade school	_____	_____
pre-teen	_____	_____
teenage	_____	_____
young adult leaving home	_____	_____
adult living life on his or her own	_____	_____

Ideally speaking, a pregnancy in marriage is not an accident but rather an event planned for and wanted by both spouses. Seen in this way, it can be said that children affect a marriage even before the first pregnancy and indeed before the marriage itself. Mature engaged couples will have frank discussions about their desire for children, when they want their first child, and how many children they want to have.

Responsible *family planning* is an integral part of every marriage. When one or both spouses are Roman Catholic, some specific considerations must be kept in mind. One of these considerations is the church's teaching on the central role that children play in God's plan for marriage.

The teaching of the church is clearly expressed in the Second Vatican Council document, *The Church in the Modern World,* in which the bishops of the Council stated:

> Marriage and conjugal love are by their nature ordained toward the begetting and educating of children. Children are really the supreme gift to marriage and contribute very substantially to the welfare of their parents. The God himself who said, "It is not good for man to be alone" (Gn 2:18) and "Who made man from the beginning male and female" (Mt 19:4), wishing to share with man a certain special participation in his own creative work, blessed male and female, saying: "Increase and multiply" (Gn 1:28). Hence, while not making the other purposes of matrimony of less account, the true practice of conjugal love, and the whole meaning of the family life which results from it, have this aim: that the couple be ready with stout hearts to cooperate with the love of the Creator and the Savior, who through them will enlarge and enrich his own family day by day (no. 50).

In putting together the Old Testament texts, "It is not good for man to be alone," and "Increase and multiply," the bishops affirmed the importance of both the intimacy between husband and wife and the children that intimacy produces. This is not to say that couples who are unable to have any children have an imperfect marriage, for as the bishops made clear:

> Marriage, to be sure, is not instituted solely for procreation; rather, its very nature as an unbreakable compact . . . persists as a whole manner and communion of life, and maintains its value and indissolubility, even when despite the often intense desire of the couple, offspring are lacking (no. 50).

But the bishops also stated that a Catholic couple should realize that openness to children is essential to being married. Parenthood is, by the will of God, a natural outcome of the romantic-sexual union of married love.

Besides this basic attitude toward children as the supreme gift of married love, there is also the practical question of *how many* children a couple decides to have. On this point, the bishops of the Council stated, "The parents themselves and no one else should ultimately make this decision in the sight of God" (no. 50).

In clarifying what is implied in making this decision in the sight of God, the bishops said:

> Let them thoughtfully take into account both their own welfare and that of their children, those already born and those which the future may bring. For this accounting they need to reckon with both the material and the spiritual conditions of the times as well as of their state in life. Finally, they should consult the interests of the family group, of temporal society, and of the church herself (no. 50).

Responsible family planning leaves the Christian couple open to deciding for themselves how many children they will have. However, a couple guided by a Christian conscience will make this decision in the light of Christian values concerning the family. This necessitates prayerful consideration of all the factors involved, such as the mental and physical health of the present family members, financial conditions and career goals.

Thus, a couple's decision to have an eighth child when they are unable to properly care for the seven they already have may well be irresponsible. So too, the decision not to have a child for trivial or purely selfish reasons may be irresponsible. A responsible decision concerning the size of the family can only grow out of self-awareness, awareness of one another, communication and a commitment to pursuing Christian goals in the marriage.

Finally, there is the question of what *method* a couple uses to control the number of children they will have. On this question, the bishops of the Council declared:

> Spouses should be aware that they cannot proceed arbitrarily, but must always be governed according to a conscience dutifully conformed to the divine law itself, and should be submissive toward

the church's teaching office, which authentically interprets that law in the light of the Gospel (no. 50).

Pope Paul VI clearly spelled out the church's present official teaching on birth control in his encyclical *Humanae Vitae* (1968). Pope Paul VI affirmed that Catholic couples who have made a *responsible* decision not to have a child at this time in their marriage may use a natural method of birth control. Natural methods are considered to be morally acceptable because they do not violate the *natural law,* that is, the God-given relationship between sexual intercourse and the conception of a child. *Humanae Vitae* regards artificial means of birth control, which include the pill, mechanical devices and sterilization, as morally wrong because they violate the natural law.

A reliable method of natural family planning that has been developed in recent years is the ovulation method. This involves a woman carefully observing several things including body temperature and the slightest changes in mucous secretion from the cervix which indicate when she is ovulating and thus capable of conceiving a child.

It has gained acceptance for several reasons: figures show it to be 99 percent effective; as a natural method it does not violate the teachings of *Humanae Vitae;* its technique calls for shared responsibility between the husband and the wife; and it appeals to those who are aware of and concerned with the effects on the body of using drugs and mechanical devices.

Although the official teaching of the church on artificial birth control is clear, the actual practice of many Catholics (approximately 80 percent in America) is to reject the church's teaching by using the pill or some other form of artificial birth control. Some Catholic theologians have also rejected the magisterium's present position on this matter. This gap or tension between official teaching and practice creates a situation described in *The American Catholic Catechism* as follows:

Since Pius XII (1951) the papal magisterium approves the calculated use of "rhythm" as a legitimate means of regulation of conception, provided the spouses have good motives for not transmitting life here and now. But since this method causes psychological and other difficulties in some cases, which can endanger the very marriage, and since it cannot be used by people of some cultural backgrounds, a number of episcopates, most moral theologians, and marriage counsellors would consider other means of contraception licit, or at least tolerable, when there is *conflict* between responsible transmission of life and the exigencies of conjugal harmony and love. Catholics have to learn to live with this pluralism in mutual respect. Meanwhile, each couple should act according to its own well-informed conscience (p. 254).

The conflict in the church today over the question of birth control is not a conflict over the holiness of sexual intimacy or the importance of children in marriage. Rather, the conflict between official church teaching and the practice of many Catholic couples concerns the question of whether the pill and other forms of artificial birth control are, in fact, morally wrong.

As the above quote suggests, those who are following the church's official teaching should avoid passing judgment on those who are not. And those couples who, in following their own carefully informed consciences, are using artificial birth control should, in turn, avoid an indifferent or flippant attitude toward church authority. The present situation calls upon all Catholic couples to deepen their faith commitment to Christ, inform their consciences through prayer and consultation, and foster an understanding of and respect for the teachings of the church.

---

1. Imagine the following: The husband feels strongly committed to following the church's official teaching against all forms of artificial birth control; the wife feels equally committed to using the pill. How would this conflict place a burden upon their marriage? In particular, how would it hinder their ability to make love in a spirit of closeness and love for one another? What

does this conflict illustrate about the need to be as open and honest as possible before marriage in discussing this sensitive and intimate matter?

2. What are some of the inevitable challenges and responsibilities that are involved in the practice of natural birth control? How could the mutual acceptance of these challenges bring a couple closer together?

3. What are some possible health hazards involved in using artificial contraceptive methods? Select volunteers to report on the latest scientific studies concerning the effects of using the pill or IUD as a contraceptive.

When Religions Differ

It is not unusual for a Catholic to marry someone of another religious tradition. The most common of these marriages involves a Catholic and a Protestant Christian. Interfaith marriages can and often do work out very well when both spouses respect one another's traditions. By such respect, each can help the other to broaden his or her understanding of what it means to be a Christian. Each can extend to the other that love which Christ demonstrated to be the essential characteristic of his followers.

However, it is unrealistic to ignore the potential for conflict in such marriages. In which church should the marriage be performed? the children baptized and raised? the family worship together as a unit?

The Catholic church does not object to a wedding between a Catholic and a Protestant Christian being performed by an ordained Protestant minister in a Protestant church. If such a wedding is arranged, the priest, at the request of the Catholic party and the invitation of the Protestant minister, will often attend and officiate at the ceremony with the minister.

The Catholic church, however, requires the Catholic party to promise to continue to practice the Catholic faith. The Catholic party must also promise to do everything possible to have the children baptized and raised Catholic. These promises are required even if the marriage ceremony itself is performed in a Protestant church.

These promises place responsibilities upon both the Catholic and non-Catholic spouses. For the Catholic, the responsibility is that of practicing the Catholic faith and raising the children Catholic. For the Protestant, the responsibility is that of accepting that he or she will be practicing his or her religion alone in a Catholic household.

Couples entering into an interfaith marriage, as with all couples, need to be as honest and open as they can be about their feelings toward religion and its place in their future marriage. Then, after they are married, they need to maintain this openness and mutual respect as they work together to achieve the goals of a happy Christian marriage.

In actual practice, some couples in an interfaith marriage do not keep the promises made before their marriage concerning raising the children Catholic. Discuss each of the following approaches to the children's religious formation:

a. not taking the children to any church until they are old enough to decide for themselves to what church, if any, they want to belong.

b. dividing the children up so that some are raised Catholic and some Protestant.

c. taking the children to both Catholic and Protestant churches and religion classes.

Communication

We will conclude this chapter with some thoughts on communication and Christian faith as two important and helpful means of fostering a happy, lasting marriage.

In Paul Tournier's insightful book, *To Understand Each Other* (John Knox Press, 1967), there is a helpful study of communication in marriage. Tournier approaches the topic of marital communication by suggesting three distinct phases in a married couple's relationship. The first phase, the honeymoon phase, is usually free of any serious problems in communication. In fact, the spouses seem to communicate very easily. Unspoken feelings are conveyed in a simple glance or embrace. Arguments are easily turned into occasion for renewed intimacy.

The second phase of marriage often begins between the fifth and 10th years. During this phase, communication problems first appear. As the first years of marriage pass, so too does the couple's blindness to each other's faults and weaknesses. The couple may realize that what they previously perceived as deep communication was, in fact, based upon an idealized and unrealistic image each had of the other and of the marriage.

Communication problems during this stage often arise because people tend to marry their opposites. A rational, logical individual may be drawn to someone who is intuitive and poetic. An outgoing and talkative person will be attracted to someone who is quiet and reserved. At first these polar differences serve to complement and round out the relationship. In this second phase of marriage, however, these differences can begin to grate on the nerves. The quiet person begins to feel that his or her spouse is a source of embarrassment at parties. The logical individual becomes frustrated at his or her spouse's "unrealistic" way of looking at life. At this stage previously unnoticed and sometimes serious faults begin to appear: drunkenness, violence, selfishness, moodiness. One or both of the spouses may feel tempted to withdraw from the relationship. At this stage, too, couples frequently think seriously of getting a divorce.

The third and most critical phase is the point at which the couple decide to respond to their painful inability to communicate with each other. Three possibilities are open to them: 1) to continue surviving together with all their mutually inflicted wounds and emotional isolation; 2) to end the marriage; or 3) to begin together to face their differences in an open and honest way and to search together for a more mature, realistic and enduring love.

Communication is one of the greatest challenges in marriage. But in a spirit of a loving, truthful search for lasting intimacy, com-

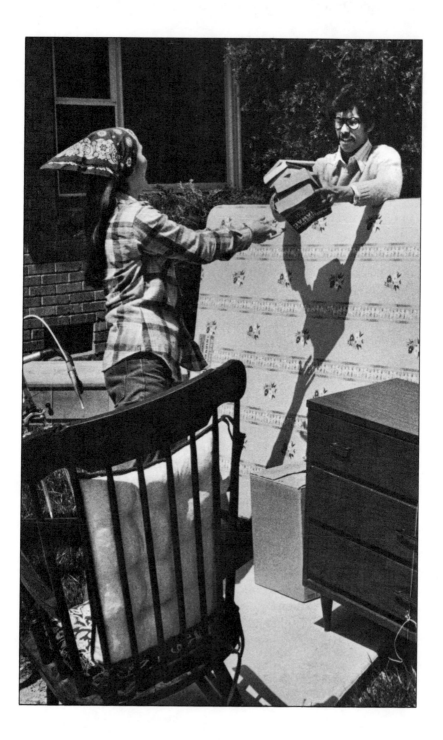

munication becomes an essential *means* of overcoming all the problems a couple may face, no matter how difficult.

1. As a class, discuss Tournier's position on marital communication.

2. Can you think of instances in which you thought you knew someone, only later to discover that you did not? How can a difference honestly faced bring a couple closer together?

3. Can you think of a time when you thought you knew yourself and later discovered you did not? Discuss the importance of Socrates' cry to "know thyself" as an essential element in learning to understand and communicate with others. How do we grow in self-knowledge?

4. As a class, discuss the following statement by Tournier on the topic of emotional incompatibility as a basis of divorce:

    > Emotional incompatibility is a myth invented by jurists short of arguments in order to plead for divorce. It is a common excuse people use in order to hide their own feelings. I simply do not believe it exists. There are no emotional incompatibilities. There are misunderstandings and mistakes, however, which can be corrected where there is the willingness to do so (p. 13).

Communication in marriage can take many forms, a few of which are listed below:

Doing things together — Sometimes love is best communicated in the sharing of some common task. Doing the dishes, painting a room, decorating a Christmas tree, or planning a trip can be moments of deep, nonverbal communication between marriage partners. Certainly the shared joys and responsibilities of raising children are one of the most important of shared activities that communicate love.

Sexual intimacy — After the honeymoon phase, sexual encounters can lose their initial thrill and physical intensity. However, as a couple's love matures so too does the capacity for more meaningful and intimate sharing through sexual union. Nor is sexual union in this sense to be understood solely in terms of full genital union in intercourse. To hold hands, embrace, dance or share other expressions of physical affection are also important in helping a couple communicate their love for one another.

Arguments — A married couple who says they *never* argue are either newlyweds or living in some kind of emotional distance or dishonesty. Of course, constant and bitter fighting is a symptom of some deep problem in the marriage. But having acknowledged this, we can say that arguing and other forms of confrontation are an important part of any mature marital relationship.

A "good argument" has several essential ingredients: first, it is an *expression of concern* over some issue rather than an attack on each other; secondly, it should be *contained* to the issue at hand. Both spouses should avoid using the argument as an occasion to dig up past failings or making general accusations ("You *always* hurt my feelings!"), for which there is no possible meaningful response.

And thirdly, the experience of many couples bears out the wisdom of the saying to "never let the sun go down on your anger." After the difference has been brought into the open, it is important for both to be anxious and willing to experience together the joys and benefits of "making up." This does not mean the difference has been overcome or that it does not have to be discussed further. But it does express the couple's conviction that the love uniting them matters more than the differences separating them.

Forgiving — An intimate exchange of love takes place when an exposed wrongdoing is met by genuine forgiveness. The experience of being truly forgiven is a *liberation* from guilt. A husband and wife are often called upon to be one another's liberators. And the honesty, the openness, the depth of encounter, the healing that can occur at such times makes forgiveness a vital form of communication in marriage. Forgiveness does not come automatically. Sometimes deception, revenge or other unworthy attitudes can block out communication. Through love a couple can meet in their common need to be set free from guilt. And meeting there, they can discover new depths to the love that makes genuine forgiveness possible.

Being present to each other — The most important form of communication is being fully present to each other. This means being more willing to listen than to talk, to be open to the point of a radical availability or vulnerability to the other's deepest needs and desires. It is the desire for a union so profound that, while remaining two unique persons, a man and woman somehow become one in the unity brought by love.

It seems that the key to communication in marriage lies neither in words nor in actions, but rather in an orientation toward *mutual loving openness and communion*. With this orientation, anything at all can communicate love: an argument, a note left taped to the refrigerator, a cup of tea shared before going to bed, an activity with the children. Without this orientation, nothing can communicate love. The most passionate sexual encounter, the most expensive gift, the most exquisite dinner can leave the couple feeling strangely alone and isolated from each other.

---

1. What are some other ways in which a married couple can communicate?

2. In some instances, a couple needs to go to a marriage counselor to learn to communicate. What are some specific situations or problems in which a marriage counselor might be needed? Why is it important to consult a marriage counselor at the beginning of communication difficulties?

3. Discuss:

> Oh, the comfort, the inexpressible comfort of feeling safe with a person; having neither to weigh thoughts nor measure words, but to pour them all out, just as they are, chaff and grain together, knowing that a faithful hand will take and sift them, keep what is worth keeping and, with the breath of kindness, blow the rest away.
>
> (George Eliot)

Christian Faith

Along with communication, Christian faith can help a couple overcome the difficulties and hardships of marriage. In fact, Christian faith and communication are closely linked. Christian faith refers to the nature or quality of the love which the spouses communicate. Christian love is essentially Christ's love, living in us through the indwelling of the Holy Spirit. Thus, the quality of love communicated in a Christian marriage has the qualities of Christ's love as its ideal.

As we saw in an earlier chapter, the Christian home is rightly called a domestic church. A Christian home is the place where husband, wife and children are invited to experience the love of Christ in and through their daily love and compassion for one another.

This crucially important point about a Christian home has been beautifully developed by Steve Landregan in the book *Marriage and the Family in a World of Change* (Ave Maria Press, 1975, Angela M. Schreiber, ed.). He suggests adapting Saint Paul's often quoted text from First Corinthians about love in the following ways:

1. Read the passage from First Corinthians (given below) aloud substituting the term "a husband" for the word "love."

2. Read the passage aloud substituting the term "a wife" for the word "love."

3. Read the passage aloud substituting the word "Christ" for the word "love."

> Love is patient; love is kind. Love is not jealous, it does not put on airs, it is not snobbish. Love is never rude, it is not self-seeking, it is not prone to anger; neither does it brood over injuries. Love does not rejoice in what is wrong but rejoices with the truth. There is no limit to love's forbearance, to its trust, its hope, its power to endure.

(1 Cor 13:4-7)

What does this exercise suggest about Christ as the source of love in a Christian marriage? What does this in turn suggest about the need for a couple in a Christian marriage to remain close to Christ through prayer and the living of a Christian life?

Finally, read the passage substituting the term "a parent" for the word "love." Discuss the significance that the Christian faith has upon the children in their growth and development into free, responsible and loving adults.

The above exercise indicates the importance of working together to build the foundation for a Christian home, a home in which the parents and the children strive together to bring alive the values of the Gospel. This involves much more than simply going to church together on Sunday. It means a daily *living* of Christian faith.

1. The situations given below might easily occur in any family. Gather into small groups and respond to each situation indicating what you think would be a *realistic, Christian* response to each situation.

   a. While at supper, one of the smaller children tells the family about a new kid in class who is mocked by everybody.

   b. The family is watching a television show which glamorizes unmarried couples living together.

   c. A racial minority family moves into the neighborhood. Most of the neighbors refuse to show welcome or friendship to the new neighbors.

   d. One parent becomes very ill and finds it extremely difficult to keep up his or her duties around the house.

   e. At Christmas time the children become completely absorbed in thinking about what presents they are going to get.

2. Do you think that television makes it more difficult to foster and develop Christian attitudes in the home? Do you think parents should censor television shows their children want to watch? To what age? Which programs? Why?

3. What do you consider to be unrealistic, unfair, or even unchristian measures parents might take in attempting to instill Christian values in the home?

SUMMARY

1. There are numerous challenges to the permanence and success of marriage today. Some of the most important of these are: incompatibility, the responsibilities of family planning and the raising of children, and religiously mixed marriages (interfaith marriages).

2. Communication is a major challenge in marriage. However, when this challenge is met in a mature and loving way, communication proves to be a basic and essential means of overcoming marital problems.

3. Communication takes many forms. In its essence, it involves the communication of love.

4. Christian faith is an effective means of overcoming marital problems.

5. Building a Christian home refers to the fostering of attitudes and actions that embody the message of the Gospel's call for us to love others as Christ loved us.

EVALUATION

Write one well-developed paragraph for each of the important points in this chapter.

CREATIVE PROJECTS

1. Interview parents or other married couples about: a) the importance of communication in marriage; b) how to develop effective channels of communication; and c) the importance of developing Christian attitudes in the home.

2. Discuss the problems and advice given in Ann Landers, Dear Abby, or a similar advice column. Pay particular attention to the values suggested in the problem, the level of communication, and the values suggested by the answer.

3. In light of all this text has said of marriage, write "Ten Commandments" for a successful and happy marriage. Do this individually. Also write an essay that explains or elaborates on these commandments. These may be shared with the class if desired.

6
The Priesthood
and the Religious Life

Then, taking bread and giving thanks, he broke it and gave it to them, saying: "This is my body to be given for you. Do this as a remembrance of me."

Lk 22:19

In this chapter, we turn from marriage to the priesthood and religious life. Since many people have only a general idea of these ways of life, we'll begin by defining each.

A priest is a man who, in a personal response to an invitation from the Holy Spirit, has received the Sacrament of Holy Orders. As a priest, he is empowered to represent Christ as celebrant of the Eucharist and to absolve sins in the Sacrament of Reconciliation. As a pastor, he leads and inspires the believing community by preaching God's word and caring for the spiritual, personal needs of the people. He is, along with his bishop, the pope (as bishop of Rome), and fellow priests and deacons a member of the *hierarchy,* which has authority to instruct the church in matters of faith and morals.

A *religious* is a man or woman who has responded to an invitation from the Holy Spirit to take vows of poverty, chastity and obedience. A religious is a member of a community of men or women dedicated to the common pursuit of personal union with God through a life of prayer and loving service to others. For most religious communities, service to others takes the form of some

119

active ministry, such as teaching, nursing, or serving the needs of the elderly or the poor. A few religious communities are cloistered, that is, strictly isolated from active involvement in the world. The ministry of these communities is to pray for the world.

This definition of the religious life allows for a distinction between diocesan or secular priests and priests who are members of a religious community. Those priests serving in most parishes are diocesan or secular priests. Although they are celibate by church law and make a promise of obedience to the bishop at their ordination, they take no vows. On the other hand, priests who are members of religious communities have taken vows. Their priestly ministry takes the form of the ministry appropriate to their community.

Thus, for example, a priest who is a Franciscan might travel about the country giving retreats; a priest who is a Jesuit might be a professor on a college campus, or a priest who is with Maryknoll might go to the foreign missions. Since most students are more familiar with diocesan priests, we will begin discussion in this chapter with their specific ministry in the church.

The church today continues to face a shortage of priests and religious. Based on the general descriptions given above, have a class discussion on why more young men and women do not express interest in these two vocations.

Besides clarifying the distinctions between priesthood and religious life, it is also worth noting the relationship of priests and religious to lay people. The church does not assert that priests or religious are called to be holier than married or single people. On the contrary, the church today stresses that marriage and the single life are vocations calling for the highest possible degree of union with God and the love of others. However, the church *does* hold up the priesthood and religious life as two forms of total dedication to Christ, which serve to remind and encourage all Christians to deepen their own faith commitment. The priesthood and religious life are two ways of life which offer the challenge to embrace a total commitment to follow Christ and love others as he has loved us.

PART I: THE PRIESTHOOD

Using the blackboard, make a list of the things a parish priest does for the people of the parish. Then discuss what the class thinks might be some of the most rewarding as well as the most challenging or difficult aspects of being a priest.

A man who decides to become a priest does so because of a conviction that he has been personally called by God to serve others, just as Christ called the first disciples:

> As he made his way along the Sea of Galilee, he observed Simon and his brother Andrew casting their nets into the sea; they were fishermen. Jesus said to them, "Come after me; I will make you fishers of men." They immediately abandoned their nets and became his followers. Proceeding a little farther along, he caught sight of James, Zebedee's son, and his brother John. They too were in their boat putting their nets in order. He summoned them on the spot. They abandoned their father Zebedee, who was in the boat with the hired men, and went off in his company. Shortly afterward they came to Capernaum, and on the sabbath he entered the synagogue and began to teach.
>
> (Mk 1:16-21)

As the Sermon on the Mount indicates, all Christians are called by Christ to "drop their nets" and "abandon their father" in an interior, spiritual sense. That is, all Christians are informed that they will not find security and happiness in their own resources or simply in human relationships, but rather they will find them in the Father as gifts of his love. Likewise, Jesus calls all Christians to minister to one another by loving others as he has loved them. (See Mt 6:19-21, 5:38-48.)

The Gospels make a distinction between the 12 apostles and the rest of Christ's disciples. Jesus' disciples numbered all who followed him. The apostles numbered only those who lived with

Jesus during the three years of his public ministry. Not only were they the first to be his disciples, but they were also the first called to a full-time commitment to share in Jesus' mission of bringing the Good News of salvation to all men and women. They were the ones sent forth by Jesus (the word "apostle" means "one who is sent") to baptize and make disciples of all nations. (See Mt 28:16-20.) Soon other apostles, such as Paul, joined the twelve in their traveling ministry of founding new Christian communities.

The priesthood as we know it today first appeared in the leaders chosen by the apostles to serve the spiritual needs of the people in each new Christian community. This continuity between today's priests and these first leaders allows us to approach the priesthood by singling out three themes in the apostles' priestly ministry which they received from Jesus, and which have been handed down through them to the priests of our own day.

These three themes are: 1) the ministry of being with others in a personal, loving way which gives witness to the presence of Jesus; 2) the ministry of leadership within the believing community, and 3) the ministry of celebrating Christ's presence in the sacraments.

The call of the apostles was an invitation to share in Christ's life and saving mission. The beautiful discourse of our Lord at the Last Supper (Jn 14-17) reveals that this sharing took the form of a deep, personal friendship between Jesus and his apostles. Jesus had touched each of the apostles in the very center of their lives. With the tragic exception of Judas, each apostle found his happiness and fulfillment in this friendship with Christ.

As the apostles traveled about with Jesus during the three years of his public ministry, they saw over and over how Jesus invited others to discover the Good News. He seemed to do this with the sick, with sinners, and outcasts whom most people tended to avoid. He stepped beyond the masks and superficialities to meet people in the very center of their life experiences, to invite them to discover in those experiences the presence of God's love and mercy. Thus, a prostitute was told she was forgiven, lepers were made clean, a woman had her dead brother returned to life, a man who had been blind from birth suddenly had sight.

The truth that emerges in Jesus' ministry is that he was a man with and for others. His way of life revealed God as being actively present and involved in people's daily lives. By the way he lived, Jesus revealed to the apostles that their call to share in his ministry would necessitate this same willingness to draw near to others. Like their master, they too would have to enter into people's lives to bring them to the awareness of the Lord's presence.

Today's priest shares in the apostles' call to bring men and women to the awareness of Christ's presence in their daily lives. If you would chart a parish priest's schedule for a typical week you would no doubt discover that he spends much of his time being with people. Some of this time is spent working with the various groups and organizations that help in parish affairs. But a great deal of his time is also spent one-on-one with others.

A priest visits the sick. He talks to engaged couples, helping them prepare for marriage. He helps parents arrange for their child's baptism. Sometimes, he helps people face a major crisis or loss, such as the death of a loved one; perhaps he simply listens to them and lets them know they are not alone in their sorrow or confusion.

The priest, in short, shares in the apostles' call to be with others as Christ's presence in the world. The strength for such a life comes from a deep, personal relationship with our Lord. In fact, a priest's life makes little sense except as a way of sharing with others the happiness and love he has found in giving himself completely to Christ. Essential to a priest's life is the call to proclaim the Gospel not simply from the pulpit but also by his presence and availability to others.

In other words, a priest's ministry is always that of evoking in others a personal awareness that they have worth and dignity as persons, that they are loved by God and that this dignity and love comes to them through Christ. This ministry is achieved not simply through what the priest says, but through the priest being a man whose own happiness, fulfillment and sense of worth come primarily from his personal relationship with Christ.

---

1. In order to better understand the priest's calling to be with others, imagine you are a priest facing each of these situations. On a scale of one to five, indicate the extent to which you would find each situation rewarding or unrewarding. (Let one equal the least rewarding, and five, the most rewarding.)

A priest is needed to help form and moderate a youth group for the high school students of the parish.

| 1 | 2 | 3 | 4 | 5 |

A girl who is a senior in high school is pregnant and is considering having an abortion.

| 1 | 2 | 3 | 4 | 5 |

A small group in the parish wants a priest to pray with them and to help them grow in their own prayer life.

| 1 | 2 | 3 | 4 | 5 |

A married couple wants help in learning how they can save their marriage from divorce.

| 1 | 2 | 3 | 4 | 5 |

A man dying of cancer wants a priest to visit him regularly in his home.

| 1 | 2 | 3 | 4 | 5 |

An engaged couple needs help preparing for marriage.

| 1 | 2 | 3 | 4 | 5 |

2. After sharing your responses to this exercise, on the blackboard make a list of the qualities or characteristics the class thinks a priest should have in order to minister effectively to others. For example, *common sense* seems to be important for anyone giving advice to others. Be sure to give reasons for each characteristic.

3. Discuss why personal prayer, making annual retreats and other forms of maintaining a close personal relationship with our Lord is essential to the life of a priest.

4. Discuss the practical necessity of study in a priest's life. Why does a priest need an in-depth knowledge of the faith in preaching and other forms of ministry? Discuss, too, the importance of recreation with friends and having some time alone in the light of the daily demands placed upon him.

Called to Minister as Leader

Jesus was the leader, the master, and teacher of the twelve apostles. He taught with authority about himself and his mission to proclaim the Kingdom of God. During his three years with the apostles, Jesus was preparing them for the leadership role they were destined to take after his death and resurrection. At the Last Supper, he washed their feet, telling them dramatically that their leadership must always be like his; namely, a way of serving and not dominating others.

After Jesus died, rose from the dead, and sent the Holy Spirit at Pentecost, the apostles went forth as ones sent by Jesus to proclaim the Good News. They spoke with authority, for the Spirit Jesus had promised to send now lived within them, moving them to serve as leaders of the new Christian communities which they founded.

A parish priest today continues to serve in a leadership role in the church. A pastor of a parish and, in larger parishes, his associate pastors, are responsible for the efficient operation of the activities of the parish community. Today, this responsibility is often shared with a parish council consisting primarily of lay people chosen from the parish. Some pastors form teams of professional lay people or perhaps a religious sister to serve the leadership needs of the parish.

What happens when a school, classroom, athletic team or any other group is given poor or inadequate leadership? Discuss leadership as a form of service to others.

In order to understand the leadership role of the parish priest, it is necessary to understand his role in relation to his bishop. Such an understanding flows from a basic understanding of how the offices of bishop, priest and deacon developed in the early Christian communities founded by the apostles.

As referred to above, the apostles had a traveling ministry that required the appointment of leaders who would live in and serve the spiritual needs of each new Christian community. There was a variety of ministries that sprang up in the early church, each of which rendered a specific service to the community. But the three positions of leadership and service which the church was eventually to regard as forming the threefold division of the priesthood were those of bishop, presbyter, and deacon.

The origin and function of the deacons are described in the Acts of the Apostles:

> In those days,
> as the number of disciples grew, the ones who spoke Greek complained that their widows were being neglected in the daily distribution of food, as compared with the widows of those who spoke Hebrew. The Twelve assembled the community of the disciples and said, "It is not right for us to neglect the word of God in order to wait on tables. Look around among your own number, brothers, for seven men acknowledged to be deeply spiritual and prudent, and we shall appoint them to this task. This will permit us to concentrate on prayer and the ministry of the word." The proposal was unanimously accepted by the community. Following this they selected Stephen, a man filled with faith and the Holy Spirit; Philip, Prochorus, Nicanor, Timon, Parmenas, and Nicolaus of Antioch, who had been a convert to Judaism. They presented these men to the apostles, who first prayed over them and then imposed hands on them. (Acts 6:1-6; also see 1 Tim 3:8-12)

Deacons and deaconesses were men and women assigned to the task of distributing food among the widows and helping with other material needs of the community. Because of the close relationship between the Eucharist and communal meals, the deacons eventually began to assist in minor ways at the celebration of the Eucharist.

The *presbyters* were the adult males who formed the community's governing body. They were chosen and appointed (Ti 1:5). As were the deacons, they were conferred in office by a ceremony referred to as the "laying on of hands" (Acts 14:23; 1 Tim 5:22). The Book of Acts tells us that the presbyters assisted the apostles at the Council of Jerusalem (15:22-23).

The *bishop's* function is difficult to distinguish from that of the presbyters at first. The bishops appeared to serve as a small group acting as a kind of executive board of presbyters. We have then an authority structure headed by a group of bishops presiding over a larger group of presbyters, who in turn were assisted in a material way by the deacons.

Around the year 110, Saint Ignatius of Antioch made the first mention of a monarchical authority structure in the church. That is, a community presided over by one bishop, instead of a group of presbyter-bishops. By the third century, the practice of having one bishop presiding over the community became the norm.

Despite the complex and uneven development of these leadership patterns we can nevertheless see a definite pattern emerge: a bishop presided over each Christian community. His primary task was to celebrate the Eucharist. The teachings given by the bishop on the word of God and Christian beliefs, especially as given at the Sunday homily, formed the focal point of the community's religious instruction. The bishop was assisted by the presbyters, whose collective wisdom and advice helped him to manage community affairs, many of which were administered by the deacons and deaconesses.

As Christianity continued to grow, small local churches were formed around the central church presided over by the bishop. By the fourth century, presbyters were serving as pastors of these small churches with authority to celebrate the Eucharist given by the bishop. Thus, by the end of the fourth century, the basic elements that form the churches' present structure of leadership were already beginning to form: each diocese presided over by a bishop, assisted by priests ordained by him to serve as pastors of the local churches of the diocese.

During this early period the papacy (that is, the notion of the pope as being leader of the entire church), first began to take a definite form. Jesus gave Peter a position of leadership among the apostles (Mt 16:13-19). Coupled to this was the early tradition that Peter founded the first Christian community in Rome. During the first two centuries following Christ's death and resurrection, the church tended to follow the organizational patterns of the Roman

Empire. As a result, the early church gradually came to consider its center to be in Rome and the bishop of Rome, as Peter's successor, and head of the entire church.

By the fifth century, the church of Rome was often consulted as a final arbiter in theological disputes. Pope Leo I (d. 461) provided the first written claim that the bishop of Rome as successor of Peter is empowered to speak on behalf of the entire church.

We see, then, the gradual development of the bishop of Rome as the head of the entire church. The bishops of the Second Vatican Council (1962) upheld this long tradition, stressing that the bishop of Rome is a sign of the church's unity. They also stressed the *collegiality of bishops,* that is, the notion that all the bishops of the church, as a group, share in the pope's office as leader and teacher of the church.

---

1. Read and discuss 1 Tim 3:1-7, in which Saint Paul writes of the high standards required of those to be chosen as bishops. Do you think Catholics today expect a similar degree of virtue in bishops and priests?

2. As the above passage makes clear, the clergy of the early church were often married. We will discuss the question of priestly celibacy later in this chapter. For now, the class can share some initial opinions on this issue: Would priests today be helped or hindered in their ministry if church law would once again allow married priests?

Called to Celebrate the Sacraments

We have reflected so far on the ministry of the parish priest in terms of being with others and serving as leader of the community. We come now to the role of the parish priest called to represent Christ in the celebration of the Eucharist and the other sacraments.

Taken in its most general sense, the term "priest" refers to a mediator between God and humanity. He is one chosen from among the people to speak to them about God. In most religions which have some type of priesthood, the priest's function as mediator takes the form of offering sacrifices to God in ritual worship.

By the time of Jesus, the Jews had a long tradition of priesthood, which centered its activities around the temple in Jerusalem. At first, neither the bishops nor presbyters were ever given the title priest. This was because the first Christians in Jerusalem were Jewish, still went to temple (Acts 2:46, 21:26), and considered the Jewish priesthood to be valid.

Gradually, however, three influences led to the formation of a Christian priesthood. First, Christians became aware that Christianity was in fact a religious tradition quite distinct from Judaism. The gradual shift away from Jerusalem toward Rome, Antioch, and other metropolitan centers, along with an increase in non-Jewish converts, added to this new awareness.

The second influence was the early Christians' growing awareness of the sacrificial nature of the Eucharist. The Letter to the Hebrews presents Jesus as a compassionate high priest, who is our mediator with the Father (see Heb 9:11-28). By the end of the first century, we find Clement of Rome and others explicitly referring to the celebrant of the Eucharist as a priest sharing in the one priesthood of Christ.

The third influence was the identification of the ministry of celebrating the Eucharist with that of the bishops and presbyters. That is, at first the bishops and presbyters were not the only ones to act as celebrant of the Eucharist. Nor does it seem that ordination by an apostle or bishop was necessary for presiding at the Eucharist. One thing is clear: whoever did preside did so because he was chosen by the community, and this communal decision amounted to a kind of ordination. Very quickly, however, acting as celebrant of the Eucharist became the exclusive privilege of the bishops and, later, the presbyters.

By the third century, a bishop was considered to be a priest, that is, someone who shared in the one priesthood of Christ by offering the sacrifice of the Eucharist. By this time also, bishops were ordaining presbyters, who by virtue of their ordinations were priests sharing in the fullness of priesthood held by the bishops. Deacons, too, were ordained by the bishop. But unlike the presbyters, they did not celebrate the Eucharist.

Gradually then, the church came to see all Christians as sharing in the one priesthood of Christ. Within this priestly people of the church, some men were called through Holy Orders to act as priests in the celebration of the Eucharist. This celebration came to be understood as being both a meal and a renewal of the sacrifice offered on the cross by Christ, who was represented in the person of the bishop or priest.

At the beginning of this chapter we pointed out that a parish priest spends a great deal of time with people by serving as leader of the parish community. In celebrating the Eucharist he celebrates with the people, the central reality of the faith—that the Risen Christ is present in the community and in the life of each of its members. Likewise, by reading the Gospel and giving the homily, the priest witnesses to the central message of his spoken ministry—that Christ loves each person and gives eternal life to all who believe in him.

The same is true, of course, when the priest celebrates baptism, marriage, reconciliation and the anointing of the sick. In these actions, he witnesses to the people that he is with them as one representing Christ alive and active in their midst.

---

1. Listed below are a number of elements which are part of an effective celebration of the Sunday Eucharist. Working either individually or in small groups, respond to each item by relating what you or the group believes to be the importance of each. After all are finished, you can share and discuss your responses as a class.

• The priest celebrating a Mass that communicates in a joyful way his faith in Christ and his desire to share that faith with the people present.

- A homily that truly applies the scripture readings to the people's daily.life in a way that they can understand and put into practice.

- Music that is well done, and which encourages the active participation of the people.

- The people being present because they want to express and experience their union with one another in Christ, rather than feeling they have to "fulfill" an obligation.

- Receiving our Lord in Communion.

- Coming on time and staying until the final hymn has been sung.

2. As a class, review the list you made earlier of things a parish priest does. In light of what you have learned, use the board to make a new and expanded list. Also discuss what the class feels might be some of the least rewarding as well as the most rewarding aspects of a priest's life.

The Priesthood Today

The priesthood today continues to undergo modifications in response to new needs arising from cultural and historical changes. The real or possible modifications which we will discuss briefly here are: the return of the permanent diaconate; priests being allowed to be married; and women being ordained to the priesthood.

Deacons

By the Middle Ages, the office of deacon had been reduced to a temporary stepping-stone for the priesthood. The reasons are complex. But one seems to be the disputes arising from the deacons' demands to celebrate the Eucharist along with the priests.

The bishops of the Second Vatican Council restored the office of permanent diaconate, primarily in response to the shortage of priests, especially in such countries as Latin America and Africa. In the United States, the permanent diaconate is open to men "of mature years" (which in practice usually means 35 years or older). These men may be married. If, however, their wives die after their ordination, they may not remarry. Rather, they must abide by the church law requiring those in Holy Orders to be celibate.

Among the tasks assigned to deacons by Pope Paul VI, the most important are:

1. Assisting bishops and priests at liturgical functions.
2. Administering baptism.
3. Reserving the Eucharist, distributing it (to himself and others), taking it to the dying, leading Eucharistic devotions.
4. Acting as the official witness at weddings when a priest cannot be present.
5. Administering sacramentals and presiding at funerals and burial services.
6. Preaching and reading the scriptures to the people.
7. Presiding at services of worship and prayer in the absence of a priest.

8. Conducting Services of the Word, especially in the absence of a priest.
9. Performing charitable and administrative duties and works of social welfare.

Discuss as a class the different ways permanent deacons assist in the needs of your diocese or local parish communities.

The Married Priest Debate

Those in favor of maintaining the present church law forbidding priests to marry point to a long tradition of priestly celibacy. We know that many of the bishops and presbyters of the early church accepted celibacy as part of their calling to ministry. As early as the Council of Nicaea (325), we find an attempt to establish mandatory celibacy for priests. By the 12th century, universally applied priestly celibacy became church law.

Those who favor celibacy point to its long tradition and to its witness value in a world so dominated by the search for sensual pleasure. They also argue that if priests were married, they would not be free to devote their full time and attention to their priestly ministry.

On the other hand, others urge that married men be able to serve as priests or even that those already ordained be allowed to marry. Those who advocate a change point to the tradition that all the apostles except John were married. Furthermore, priests were permitted to marry until the Middle Ages, when a church law obliged celibacy. In other words, there is nothing incompatible between priesthood and marriage. Those promoting this change also point out that celibacy in the early church was considered to be a *charism,* a freely given gift of the Spirit. To impose a charism as a law seems contrary to the nature of freely given gifts. As a shortage of priests continues along with a growing sensitivity to the holiness of marriage, some say the time has come to allow married men to serve the church as priests.

Have a class discussion to determine the class's beliefs on this issue.

The Women Priest Debate

Another debate surrrounding the priesthood today is the ordination of women. Arguments supporting the present practice of an all-male priesthood point to the fact that Jesus called only men to be apostles. Even his mother was not included in the apostles' priestly ministry. Furthermore, in her nearly 2000 years, the church has carefully maintained this tradition. Adding to its strength is the notion that the ordained priest must be able to represent Christ physically (as a man) as well as spiritually. Thus, some hold that the church could not change this tradition established by Christ himself even if it wanted to.

On the other hand, those in favor of the ordination of women to the priesthood hold that an all-male priesthood violates human dignity as well as women's baptismal call to share fully in the life of the church. These same groups also point out that scripture does not expressly forbid women to be priests. The fact that Christ chose an all-male priesthood is due, say these groups, to the social, historical conditions in which he lived and which made women subservient to men. The theologians of the church (for the most part all men) have also been subject to similar sociologically and culturally derived assumptions about women.

Those in favor of women priests are asking if it is not time to break out of this mold. Do we not have a new awareness of the equality of women? And should not this equality be expressed in a bold and courageous way by the church, by allowing women to exercise their right as baptized Christians to minister to the church as ordained priests?

Discuss the feelings of the class regarding the ordination of women.

PART II: THE RELIGIOUS LIFE

> *". . . everyone who has given up home, brothers and sisters,*
> *father and mother, wife and children or property, for my*
> *sake will receive many times as much and inherit everlasting*
> *life."*
>
> Mt 19:20

Our reflections on the religious life will be divided into three parts: 1) a look at the three vows of poverty, chastity and obedience as seen from the perspective of the New Testament, 2) a brief overview of some of the major developments in the history of the religious life, and 3) a brief examination of some of the contemporary concerns affecting religious life. We will conclude with the steps to be taken by those who feel God may be calling them to the priesthood or religious life.

> *Before we begin, it might be helpful to turn back to the*
> *brief description of the religious life given at the beginning of this chapter.*

The New Testament Origins of the Three Vows

The religious life has often been presented by those who live it as an attempt to preserve the spirit of the *apostolic life,* that is, the way of life lived by the apostles and the first Christians immediately following Pentecost. An account of this way of life is given in the Acts of the Apostles:

> They devoted themselves to the apostles' instruction and the communal life, to the breaking of bread and the prayers. A reverent fear overtook them all, for many wonders and signs were performed by the apostles. Those who believed shared all things in common; they would sell their property and goods, dividing everything on the basis of each one's need. They went to the temple area together every day, while in their homes they broke bread. With exultant and sincere hearts they took their meals in common, praising God and winning the approval of all the people. Day by day the Lord added to their number those who were being saved.
>
> (Acts 2:42-47)

The above passage portrays a community of men and women enthusiastic about their faith in the risen Lord, who celebrated his presence in the breaking of the bread. Since their master had made their love for one another to be the measure of their love for him, they shared their goods in common. Ideally, no one would lack any basic necessities.

The notion of charism is basic to the spirit of the apostolic life. A charism is a gift given an individual, enabling that person to witness to Christ and to serve the community in a specific way. St. Paul, for example, tells the Corinthians that the one Lord, whose loving presence fills the whole community, touches each person in a unique way. To one he gives the charism of preaching, to another healing, and to still another the gift of teaching (see 1 Cor 12).

Because a charism is from the risen Lord, the person who possesses it witnesses to the presence of Jesus actively at work within the community. Those who preached, for example, gave witness to Christ proclaiming the Good News to his people. Those given the charisms of being a bishop, presbyter or deacon witnessed to the risen Lord leading and serving the community. The martyrs (the word "martyr" means "witness") witnessed to Jesus by inviting his followers to share in his resurrection through sharing in his death. A charism, then, expresses a specific way of imitating Christ and thus making his presence known and felt within the community.

Charisms were also closely related to the kingdom of God that Jesus was to establish. Jesus taught that that kingdom is already here and is expressed whenever one person loves and serves another. Some charisms witnessed to this "here and now" aspect of the kingdom. Most people in the apostolic community, for example, were married men and women with children. They were called upon to witness to the kingdom by the charisms of fidelity and marital love, which reveals Christ's presence in the home. Similarly, deacons witnessed to the kingdom of God by serving Jesus present in the poor.

But Christ also promised to return at the end of time to establish his Father's kingdom of eternal justice and love (Mk 13:24-29). Other charisms witnessed to this final, eternal aspect of the kingdom of God. The martyr, for example, was held in high esteem by the early Christian community. By dying for Christ, martyrs directed the Christian community's awareness beyond space and time to the eternal happiness promised by Christ.

Closely related to the martyr were those who embraced a life of voluntary poverty and celibacy. Those who vowed poverty witnessed to the eternal treasure awaiting those who left all things to follow Jesus (Mt 19:27-30). Those who embraced voluntary celibacy witnessed to the coming of God's kingdom, which Jesus likened to a wedding between ourselves and the Father (Mt 25:1-13). Those who received and accepted the charisms of martyrdom, voluntary poverty and celibacy reminded all in the community of the final promise and mystery awaiting every follower of Christ.

1. As a class, look at the differences and similarities that can be seen in comparing the spirit of the apostolic community with the spirit of a modern parish. For example, discuss how people today share their goods with the poor and how the charisms of teaching or reading God's word are expressed in the liturgy.

2. Quietly and slowly read the Sermon on the Mount (Mt 5-7). As a class, discuss the following:

   a) What would it be like living in a community of men and women who have sincerely based their lives on the Sermon on the Mount? What elements in a family, parish or school are obstacles to the realization of such a community?

   b) Which teachings of Jesus seem to you to be the most attractive? the most difficult? the most important?

3. In a similar fashion, as a class read and then discuss Jesus' discourse at the Last Supper (Jn 14-17).

   a) Which verses speak to you most strongly of Jesus' love for his followers?

   b) What response of love does Jesus ask for from his followers? Discuss the Sermon on the Mount as the perfect model for a response of love to Christ.

   c) Why is prayer important for anyone sincerely seeking to be a follower of Christ? What does this suggest about the importance of the Eucharist in the life of any Christian community?

The class may want to put together a Scripture prayer service with readings taken from the discourse at the Last Supper and the Sermon on the Mount.

The Three Vows

With this background, we can now reflect on vows of poverty, chastity and obedience as lived by contemporary religious. Thus, we can see how each contributes to the charism of witnessing to Christ in the world today.

Poverty

The vow of poverty is made in imitation of Christ who, during his life on earth, was a poor man. His earthly father, Joseph, was a simple carpenter. During his public ministry, Jesus did not even have a simple dwelling he could call his own. At his death, soldiers gambled for the clothes off his back.

The *charism* witnessing to this aspect of Jesus and his message is rooted in the Gospel story of the rich young man who asked Jesus how he could find eternal life. Jesus responded by telling him to keep the commandments. The rich young man replied that he already kept them, but wanted to know what more he could do. Jesus then told him, "If you seek perfection, go sell your possessions, and give to the poor. You will then have treasure in heaven" (see Mt 19:16-22).

When a man or woman today takes a vow of poverty as a member of a religious community, he or she is embracing the charism of poverty offered by Christ to the rich young man. In imitation of Christ, the religious is committed to a simple lifestyle in matters of food, clothing and other necessities. By taking a vow of poverty, the religious renounces the right to own private property. Everything the religious uses belongs not to the individual person but to the community. This charism does not imply that acquiring and enjoying material things and the money to buy them is immoral. On the contrary, married people are duty-bound to make money and acquire material property in order to care for their family. Those who take a vow of poverty, however, can be witnesses to all Christians that making money and acquiring material things cannot be the center of life.

The renunciation of the right to own private property means little if anything without a corresponding inner renunciation of the self-centeredness and false securities which material possessions can sometimes represent. In other words, the vow of poverty also witnesses to a healthy forgetfulness of self that allows the religious to become more completely concerned about others and their needs.

---

1. Discuss as a class the witness value of living the vow of poverty in our society today.

2. Discuss the ways in which a possessive or self-centered attitude can prevent us from being sensitive and responsive to the needs of others. How can such attitudes make us the slaves of our own possessions?

3. Read and discuss the following Scripture passages, indicating what insights they give you about Jesus' teachings regarding poverty:

    Lk 12:13-34   Lk 16:9-15   Mt 6:19-34

Chastity

The vow of chastity is made in imitation of Christ, who never married. This in no way implies that Jesus was not capable of experiencing sexual feelings and desires. Nor does it mean that Jesus shied away from women. In fact, the Gospels tell us that many of his followers were women, and that he sometimes surprised his disciples with the openness with which he spoke to women. Nor does Jesus' teaching have any kind of anti-sexual or anti-marriage overtones.

Jesus himself chose not to marry and he invited those to whom the gift was given to do the same:

> Not everyone can accept this teaching, only those to whom it is given can do so. Some men are incapable of sexual activity from birth; some have deliberately been made so; and some there are who have freely renounced sex for the sake of God's reign. Let him accept this teaching who can.
> (Mt 19:11-12)

Since St. Paul was unmarried for the sake of the kingdom, he urged those who were not married to remain so (1 Cor 7:8-10, 25-28). The charism of consecrated celibacy quickly became recognized as a sign of total dedication to Christ in the community.

The renunciation of a spouse and family calls for a freely chosen renunciation of the most basic forms of human love and companionship. This in itself witnesses to the tremendous value of what the religious freely chooses in place of marriage; namely, his or her relationship with Christ. This does not mean the religious loves Christ instead of loving others. Rather, it means the religious is called to love others in and through this total commitment to Christ. The renunciation of family life extends the love of the religious beyond the confines of an immediate family. The religious is thus a sign of the love which Christ has for all people.

The great majority of Christians are called to follow Christ in and through the daily rewards and challenges of married life. The religious who takes a vow of chastity witnesses to all Christians that true love always transcends pleasure. The religious who finds happiness and love while renouncing marriage is a sign that married love and all other human ties are but a faint shadow of the love God will fully reveal to us when we enter into his kingdom.

What values or attitudes prevalent in today's society might make it more difficult for a young person to accept the charism of the vow of chastity? In what way could these same values and attitudes give the vow of chastity an even greater witness value?

Obedience

The vow of obedience is made in imitation of Christ, who was always obedient to the will of his Father. The apostles were the first to witness to the charism of sharing in this obedience of Christ by obeying Christ as the source of the Father's will in their lives.

The significance of the vow of obedience is suggested in the Latin word *ob-audire* meaning "to listen carefully." To vow obedience means to listen carefully for the will of God in each situation. Christ is the perfect model of this listening. His public life began with a period of 40 days alone in the desert. The Gospels tell us, too, that he often spent whole nights alone in prayer and that he often prayed before performing a miracle.

The religious seeks to imitate this same attentiveness to the will of the Father. In practical terms, this means making all major decisions in dialogue with the will of one or more superiors in the community. With his or her superiors, the religious attempts to discern which course of action is the will of God.

The vow of obedience witnesses to all Christians their need to pray, "listen" and reflect before making any major decisions. The charism of obedience gives witness to the paradox that true freedom is found in seeking to do the will of God in all things.

What would be some examples of major decisions that lie ahead for young men and women finishing high school? Discuss as a class what it might mean to seek to do God's will in facing these decisions?

Brief History of Religious Life

The history of the religious life as a distinct lifestyle began in the second and third centuries when men and women went into the deserts of Egypt, Palestine, Arabia and Persia to seek God through a life of prayer and penance. By far the most widely known of these monks or hermits was St. Anthony of Egypt.

Anthony was born of wealthy parents near the town of Memphis, Egypt, about the year 250 A.D. His life was suddenly changed when he heard the Gospel story about the rich young man who was told by Christ to sell all his possessions and to follow him. In response to this Gospel passage, Anthony felt the need to imitate the rich young man by giving away all his land and money to go into the desert to seek God.

Anthony went into the desert about the year 270 A.D. At first he lived in an empty tomb on the edge of the city. He soon went deeper into the desert, where he lived in a deserted fort. He stayed there for 20 years, devoting his life to prayer and self-denial. He rarely left his place of solitude, except to visit and console inmates in nearby prisons. Soon his reputation as a man of God spread throughout the area. Other men came, asking if they could live near Anthony, imitating his way of life and turning to him for advice in the pursuit of God.

The growing number of hermits eventually prompted Anthony to leave with only two companions to go even deeper into the desert. He eventually settled in a small, deserted oasis in upper Thebes, where he lived until his death at the age of 105. He left behind him the first form of religious community consisting of a small group of hermits. These hermits lived alone, but near others who gathered around a master or spiritual guide.

A short time later in this same area, St. Pachomius and St. Basil were responsible for bringing groups of hermits together to live under a common rule in a monastery. The rule of St. Basil is still followed to this day in some monasteries of the Eastern rite church.

This movement to the desert can, in part at least, be attributed to the effects of Constantine's Edict of Milan (313 A.D.), which ended the persecution of Christians. As the church began to grow under its new freedom, those who went into the desert felt that the church had lost the original zeal of the apostolic life. The hermit was called the martyr's little brother, indicating that the life of the hermit was considered to be a mystical death or total surrendering of self to Christ. Another factor in the success of the desert movement was the influence of neo-Platonic thought, which emphasized the invisible, mystical aspects of human nature. The third and

fourth centuries were a time of an extraordinary emergence of men and women who went into the desert to live a form of religious life. Its key themes were poverty, chastity, obedience, solitude, charity to others and mystical union with God.

---

1. The biblical models which were frequently used to exemplify the hermit way of life are: Elijah (1 Kgs 17-19), John the Baptist (Mt 3), Mary sitting at the feet of Jesus (Lk 10:38-42) and the apostles with Jesus at the transfiguration (Mt 9:2-8). The class can read the biblical passages about these figures and events and then discuss what they reveal about the hermits' ideals and way of life.

2. The sayings of the desert fathers, as the hermits were called, were treasured by the Christians, who read them and were inspired by the hermits' way of life. A few of these sayings are given below. As a class, discuss what you think each saying reveals about the attitudes and ideals of the desert fathers. (Quotes are taken from Thomas Merton, *The Wisdom of the Desert*, New York: New Directions, 1960.)

The same Father (Abbot Pastor) said: If there are three monks living together, of whom one remains silent in prayer at all times, and another is ailing and gives thanks for it, and the third waits on them both with sincere good will, these three are equal, as if they were performing the same work.

One of the elders was asked what was humility, and he said: If you forgive a brother who has injured you before he himself asks pardon.

Abbot Pastor said: Any trial whatever that comes to you can be conquered by silence.

The same Abbot Agatho would say: Even if an angry man were to revive the dead, he would not be pleasing to God because of his anger.

Blessed Marcarius said: This is the truth, if a monk regards contempt as praise, poverty as riches, and hunger as a feast, he will never die.

Abbot Lot came to Abbot Joseph and said: Father, according as I am able, I keep my little rule, and my little fast, my prayer, meditation and contemplative silence; and according as I am able I strive to cleanse my heart of thoughts: now what more should I do? The elder rose up in reply and stretched out his hands to heaven, and his fingers became like ten lamps of fire. He said: Why not be totally changed into fire?

St. Athanasius brought word of St. Anthony of Egypt and his way of life to Rome, where it proved to be a stimulus to the rise of monastic life in the West. By far the most significant figure in Western monasticism was St. Benedict (480?-547? A.D.). After studying in Rome, he lived as a hermit on Mount Subiaco in Italy. Soon, in a manner similar to Anthony, he began to be approached by men who wanted to imitate his way of life, live near him, and have him be their spiritual guide.

As the numbers of those who approached him grew, he gathered his followers into monasteries and wrote a rule. As the years went by, Benedictine monasteries spread throughout all of Europe. In the Dark Ages following the fall of the Roman Empire, Benedictine monasteries became practically the sole surviving centers of culture and education in the West. It would be difficult to overestimate the importance and influence of monks and the monastic life on the life of the church during the entire period of the Middle Ages.

Later, different orders of monks such as the Carthusians, Cistercians and Camaldoli began to appear. Beneath this diversification, however, there was a unified set of principles and ideals which formed the basis for this first form of religious life, which still continues to exist in the church. Some of these principles and ideals are briefly listed below.

- *The vows:* to live in imitation of Christ through voluntary poverty, chastity and obedience.

- *Interior transformation:* to seek holiness—a purifying of one's deepest attitudes and thoughts through prayer, self-denial and charity toward others.

- *Physical separation from secular society:* to live in isolation from the world for the sake of praying for the world and as a sign of renouncing the false values that are commonly found there.

- *Life of prayer:* to give one's whole life over to union with God in deep meditation and liturgical prayer, with the belief that there is power in prayer to touch and heal the sufferings of this world.

The bishops of the Second Vatican Council (1962-65) stated that the life of men and women following Christ in seclusion from the world in some form of the monastic life continues to be important in the church today:

> Communities which are entirely dedicated to contemplation, so that their members in solitude and silence, with constant prayer and and penance willingly undertaken, occupy themselves with God alone, retain at all times, no matter how pressing the needs of the active apostolate may be, an honorable place in the Mystical Body of Christ, whose "members do not all have the same function" (Rm 12:4). For these offer to God a sacrifice of praise which is outstanding. Moreover, the manifold results of their holiness lend luster to the people of God which is inspired by their example and which gains new members by their apostolate which is as effective as it is hidden (*Decree on the Adaptation and Renewal of the Religious Life,* n.7).

As a class, discuss why we in America today are likely to have a difficult time relating to the monastic way of life.

Religious in the Midst of the World

While monastic communities served many needs of the church well, there arose the awareness of the need for some religious to go beyond the monastic walls. St. Francis and St. Dominic each founded new religious orders which brought about a new form of religious life lived in the midst of the secular world. St. Francis (born in 1182 in Italy) had little formal education. In his youth he was known for his ability to spend his father's money, eating and drinking with his friends.

Francis' life was radically changed by a deep religious experience which moved him to sell all his belongings and to live in extreme poverty. Francis did not isolate himself in a monastery. Rather, he went about barefoot preaching a simple message: "Fear and honor God, praise him and bless him. . . . Repent . . . for you know not how soon you will die. . . . Abstain from evil, persevere in the good."

Francis was one of the great mystics of the church. He often spent whole nights in prayer. On several occasions, he was seen lifted up off the ground in a state of deep meditation. On September 14, 1224, after a night spent in prayer, Francis received the stigmata, that is, the wounds of Christ in his hands, feet and side; these remained until his death in 1226. He left behind him a vast number of Franciscan friars who, inspired by his example, lived the religious life in the midst of the world.

St. Dominic was born in Spain in the year 1170. As a youth, he chose a life of voluntary poverty. He was known primarily for his gift of preaching. He eventually settled in Rome, where he inspired others to lead a life of the vows and the preaching of the Gospel. By his death in 1221, the potential impact of his genius could already be seen. Within a few years, Dominican friars had established themselves as scholars in the great learning centers of Europe.

The Franciscan and Dominican orders founded by Sts. Francis and Dominic were in a sense built upon the principles of the monks living in monasteries. Franciscans and Dominicans lived the vows, sought an interior transformation through prayer, self-denial and charity to others, and they emphasized the importance of a new openness toward the world. Unlike the monks, the friars did not live in isolation from others. On the contrary, they roamed about through the towns and villages preaching God's word. As time went on, the Dominicans and the Franciscans represented the two leading intellectual schools of thought of the Middle Ages.

The Clerics Regular

In its beginnings the religious life was essentially a lay movement. That is, in general, religious were not members of the clergy but rather laymen dedicated to seeking God. Gradually, however, the veneration given to priests prompted the ordination of large numbers of men in religious communities. As part of this trend, there began to appear a new type of religious life known as the clerics regular, consisting of communities of priests living under the vows of poverty, chastity and obedience.

Probably the most influential of these later groups is the Society of Jesus, usually referred to as the Jesuits, founded by St. Ignatius of Loyola (1471-1556). The Jesuits put themselves at the service of the pope to be sent throughout the world to teach and preach God's word. The Jesuits have become known for their scholarship, staffing such universities as Fordham and Georgetown in the United States.

Congregations of Simple Vows

When someone enters one of the major religious orders of the church, he or she is first called a postulant, a term meaning "one who seeks admission." After a period of a few months, the postulant receives the religious habit of the order and becomes a novice. During the novitiate, the novice learns about the life he or she is considering as a life choice. The novitiate period lasts one or two years and ends with the taking of simple, temporary vows. After the one- to three-year period of temporary vows has expired, the individual either leaves the religious life and returns to the world or takes final, solemn vows which are binding until death.

The Jesuits introduced permanent, simple vows; that is, vows made without the liturgical solemnity of the solemn vows taken by the religious orders. This custom was soon followed by a great number of religious congregations, such as the Passionists and the Redemptorists.

Each stage of the religious life lived by men had a corresponding movement led and lived by women. Women became hermits in the second and third centuries. St. Benedict's twin sister, St. Scholastica, began Benedictine monasteries for women just as St. Clare, friend of Francis of Assisi, started the Poor Clares, an order of cloistered religious for women. Many women likewise

started congregations of simple vows. Many of these groups were devoted to specific ministries such as the education of young children, nursing the sick, or caring for orphans. One of the most recent of such congregations is the one formed by Mother Teresa of Calcutta, devoted to caring for the lepers, the sick and the dying of India.

Listed below are a number of ministries in which religious today are active. On a scale of 1 to 5 (with 1 representing the least and 5 the most) indicate the degree to which you feel you would find each ministry to be personally fulfilling.

| 1 | 2 | 3 | 4 | 5 |

Serving the poor in a small village in the foreign missions.

| 1 | 2 | 3 | 4 | 5 |

Caring for terminal cancer patients.

| 1 | 2 | 3 | 4 | 5 |

Working with emotionally disturbed teenagers.

| 1 | 2 | 3 | 4 | 5 |

Teaching at a university.

| 1 | 2 | 3 | 4 | 5 |

Teaching high school.

| 1 | 2 | 3 | 4 | 5 |

Working in a drug rehabilitation center in a poverty area of a city.

After sharing and discussing your responses as a class, discuss why personal prayer and the support of others in the community would be important in effectively carrying out these ministries.

The Religious Life Today

The changes affecting the religious life today are primarily the result of the Second Vatican Council's decree calling for the renewal of the religious life. A second related cause is the steep decline in religious vocations and the exodus of those in religious life, both of which occurred in the 1960s and 70s. Three basic movements of renewal appeared as a consequence of these and other causes; namely, a return to the spirit of the founder, modernization and concern for the personal fulfillment of the individual religious.

In terms of a return to the spirit of the founder, many religious orders and congregations attempted to clarify the original spirit with which their founder first brought their community into existence. A return to this spirit often resulted in a return to a simpler lifestyle, with more attention given to community and private prayer.

The movement toward modernization affected many of the externals of the religious life. Until the renewal following the Council, for example, some monastic orders still wore medieval underwear and performed public penances. Many congregations, especially of women, wore habits that were in some cases uncomfortable and impractical. These and other similar practices were either dropped or modified to conform to the spirit of our own times. Sometimes the changes went beyond externals and called for a prudent reinterpretation of the founder's teachings in the light of contemporary needs and developments.

The movement toward a concern for the personal fulfillment of the individual religious can be approached under the headings of each of the three vows:

Poverty: Some religious felt the need to clarify the nature of their vow of poverty. In doing so, some had difficulties with the possible discrepancy between a life of poverty and the large and sometimes luxurious buildings owned by some orders and congregations. In response to this concern, some religious have moved into small houses with two or three companions in an attempt to live a simpler lifestyle.

Before the renewal, spurred by the Second Vatican Council, a religious' travel costs, dental bills and other personal expenses were all more or less automatically paid through a community office. Today, however, many communities have adopted the practice of giving each religious a small, fixed sum of money each month with which he or she must care for financial needs. This helps the religious experience poverty in a way that comes closer to the financial limitations of many poor married and single people living in the world.

Chastity: Much of the attention given by religious to the vow of chastity since the Council has focused on the emotional, psychological fulfillment that should go hand in hand with this expression of commitment to the Gospel. There is a stress today on a religious being like every human being—a sexual being whose masculinity or femininity should be enhanced by the commitment he or she has made.

Not being married inevitably involves a sense of loneliness and the realization that one lives without the love and intimacy of a spouse and children. This realization is part of the sacrifice which gives the vow of chastity its meaning. For what is sacrificed should increase the capacity of religious to love others and experience many kinds of friendship and human companionship.

Obedience: Before the renewal of the religious life, members of communities were often expected to ask permission for such minor things as a new pair of shoelaces or taking a nap when feeling ill. Today religious communities are stressing the need for the religious to function as free, responsible adults capable of a more mature approach to the vow of obedience.

In more serious matters, religious are encouraged to enter into dialogue with their superiors, "to listen carefully" together to the signs of God's will in a given situation. Such an approach stresses that the vow of obedience calls for more and not less of an active, personal responsibility in facing decisions.

Break up into small groups. Each group should put together a list of five elements of the religious life that everyone agrees would be fulfilling and rewarding. Make a similar list of five items noting what the group feels would be difficult or especially challenging about living the religious life. When all are finished, you can share and discuss your responses with the whole class.

Inquiring Into a Priestly or Religious Vocation

Three steps are often suggested for those who think they may have a vocation to the priesthood or religious life.

Inquire: First, it is necessary to gather information about the priesthood and religious life. This is usually done by talking to a priest or a religious, or writing to the vocations director of the seminary or religious community to which one feels he or she may be called to enter. The process often entails an inquiry on the part of the seminary or religious community into the qualifications of the applicant. In general, these include such elements as a sincere desire to do God's will, good physical and emotional health, and, in the case of the priesthood, the ability to handle seminary studies in philosophy, scripture, moral and systematic theology and pastoral theology.

Pray and Reflect: After learning about the priesthood or religious life, it is necessary to pray and reflect, asking for God's guidance in making the right decision. Becoming a priest or religious is not like joining a social club or going into a certain line of work. It is instead a deep and lasting commitment to give oneself to others in the name of Christ. Such a commitment can be made only in a spirit of prayerful openness to God and his will in one's life.

Act: It becomes necessary at some point to put one's inquiry, prayer and reflection into action. This means either setting aside considerations of a priestly or religious vocation or entering the seminary or religious community to which one feels drawn. This entrance into a seminary or a religious community does not, of course, constitute any kind of final commitment. On the contrary, the time of seminary training and novitiate are periods intended to give the applicant the time and experience necessary to make an enlightened decision to leave or make a commitment at the time of ordination or vows.

SUMMARY

1. A priest is called by the Holy Spirit to be with others in a way that witnesses to the presence of Christ, to serve the community as leader and to represent Christ in the celebration of the Eucharist and the other sacraments.

2. The role of bishops, priests and deacons in the church today is directly related to the role of bishop, presbyter and deacon in the early church.

3. The pope as bishop of Rome and successor of St. Peter holds a unique place among the bishops as leader of the church.

4. The charism of voluntary poverty and chastity in the apostolic community witnessed to the presence of Christ and the coming of God's kingdom.

5. The religious life as a distinct lifestyle based on the three vows of poverty, chastity and obedience first appeared in the third and fourth centuries with an emphasis on personal union with God through prayer, penance and charity toward others.

6. Later, in the 12th century, the Franciscans and Dominicans initiated a way of religious life that introduced a more active involvement in the world.

7. Those who feel God may be calling them to the priesthood or religious life need to inquire, pray and reflect, and then act.

EVALUATION

A. Write a short essay covering the main aspects of a priest's ministry in a parish. Include the historical basis for each aspect of priestly ministry.

B. Write a short essay covering the nature of the three vows taken by religious. Include some historical background pertinent to each vow.

CREATIVE PROJECT

1. Ask a diocesan priest and one or more religious to come in on different days to speak to the class.

2. Have a group in the class find out which religious communities have houses or institutions in your diocese. The group can then report its findings to the class.

RESEARCH PROJECT

Select one of the founders of a religious order or congregation listed below. After presenting a brief biography of the person selected, write a historical study of the community founded by the person selected:

St. Basil
St. Benedict
St. Scholastica
St. Francis of Assisi
St. Clare
St. John Bosco

St. Bruno
St. Romuald
St. Alphonsus Liguori
St. Teresa of Avila
Mother Teresa of Calcutta

7
The Single Life

The unmarried man is busy with the Lord's affairs, concerned with pleasing the Lord . . .
1 Cor 7:32

In this chapter we will examine the single life. That is, we will reflect on the way of life followed by those who do not marry or who do not commit themselves to the priesthood or religious life.

Models of the Single Life

The single life covers an extremely wide range of situations and lifestyles. The swinging playboy bachelor and the aging spinster are both single. So is the college student planning to marry after graduation and the woman with four children whose husband suddenly died of a heart attack. We will begin by discussing some of the most common forms of the single life.

The Young Adult

Most young men and women in their late teens are single, and many remain single until at least their early or mid-twenties. Generally speaking, young men and women live the single life on a temporary basis to give them time to be ready for the lifetime commitment of marriage. The young adult, for example, often goes through a period of higher education or special training after high school. There is also the need to grow socially by getting to know and dating a variety of members of the opposite sex in order to meet and finally commit oneself for life to one person.

Even without any direct reference to marriage, the single life of the young adult is an important time for personal growth and development. It is a time to explore life and new ideas, to learn about oneself and others. The young single adult is free to travel, to study, to try new kinds of work; in short, to choose one's own path in life. It is this freedom that motivates some young adults to postpone marriage. But the single young adult also feels the deep need to share one's life path with a partner. And it is this need for intimacy that contributes toward the eventual decision of most young adults to marry.

1. As a class, list on the board some of the questions and challenges that face young adults as they leave home to go to college.

2. Discuss the pros and cons of continuing to live at home after graduation from high school.

3. Considering the above presentation, do you feel that a couple who meet and fall in love toward the end of the senior year of high school should still wait several years before getting married?

Single for the Sake of a Career

Some men and women choose to postpone marriage because they feel the obligations of marriage and family life would interfere with their dreams of succeeding in a career. A woman, for example, may want very much to become an executive in a large corporation. A man may want to become a surgeon. Or a person might be committed to some form of the arts, such as music or acting, which often does not pay enough money or offer enough stability to support marriage and family life.

1. What are some other careers that might easily make a person decide to postpone marriage?

2. What circumstances would make choosing a career over marriage selfish? What are some examples of how a total dedication to a career could be a way of loving and serving others?

The Widowed and Divorced

Many people get married and perhaps live the married life for many years, only to lose their spouse through a broken marriage or the death of their spouse. Of course, in many ways, the situation of the divorced and separated and the widow and widower is quite different. The church may view the divorced or separated Catholic as still married and he or she faces a different kind of loss and subsequent readjustment than do those who lose their spouse because of death.

It is not at all uncommon for a woman who married at 18 to lose her husband through death at age 50, then live the single life until her death perhaps 20 or 30 years later. Just as all who are married prepared for marriage by first living the single life, many married people return to the single life and perhaps may live as a single adult for more years than they were married.

1. As a class, discuss the various situations in which it seems desirable or undesirable to remarry after the death of one's spouse. For example, consider the question of remarriage for a 30-year-old man with four small children as compared to a 65-year-old woman whose children have left home and married.

2. Earlier, we discussed the single life of the young adult as a time for exploring new life experiences. Discuss the single life after marriage as also being a time for new life experiences.

Single for Life

Some people never marry, but remain single all their lives. Usually, this is not due to any rejection of marriage, but to a series of events or circumstances over which the individual has little or no control. For example, some people who postponed even considering marriage during their twenties discover that in their thirties they have become attached to their privacy and independence. Others simply do not find the right person at the right time, or break a long engagement and then never find anyone else they wish to marry. Still others remain single because they have a sick parent or other family commitments which they feel do not leave them free to marry.

Regardless of the reasons for not marrying, the permanently single adult, like everyone, must come to terms with the reality of his or her situation. That is, the single adult must learn to enhance the rewarding possibilities of being single, and, at the same time, cope in a responsible way with the inevitably difficult moments which are part of going through life as a single adult.

1. What are some other reasons people remain single all their lives?

2. Take a moment and consider the possibility of living the rest of your life as single adults. Then write a list of images, descriptive words or feelings that come to mind. Share your responses by listing them on the board and discussing them as a class.

3. Sometimes people who live as single adults for a number of years eventually marry. How do you think getting married at 45 differs from getting married at 25? In the class discussions consider the following: 1) the degree of maturity and ability to appreciate one another, 2) problems of adjustments, 3) having children.

Loneliness: A Challenge for the Single Adult

Being single is often seen as a lonely life. There is a considerable degree of truth in such a notion. The single adult who daily returns home from work to face an empty apartment, and who sleeps alone each night, will most likely experience more loneliness than the married person who comes home to a loving family. But, in acknowledging the loneliness that inevitably accompanies the single life, it is necessary to consider it in a proper perspective.

Loneliness, for example, is not to be equated with *being alone.* Loneliness is the unpleasant and sometimes painful feeling of being alone when we do not want to be. But being alone is sometimes a desirable condition because it can give us the breathing space we need just to be ourselves. This is, in fact, one of the potentially rewarding aspects of the single life.

A second consideration is the fact that everyone at times feels lonely. Everyone has experienced, at least momentarily, the wave of loneliness which can come without warning in a crowded room or on a busy street. Every married couple has at times experienced the loneliness of being unable to share some strong need or emotion. In other words, loneliness is not a curse put on those who are single. It is rather a universal human experience inseparable from life itself.

Although it might be unpleasant to experience, loneliness in the single life does not have to be a complete negative. On the contrary, by learning to live with, to understand and accept their own loneliness, single adults can arrive at a deeper understanding of themselves and others. The single person can also be more appreciative and aware of the moments of love and union with others that come into their lives. Loneliness is then not simply an unpleasant feeling, but a challenge which offers the potential for a richer and more meaningful life, if the person is willing to face it.

A distinction can be made between *emotional* and *social* loneliness in the single life. *Emotional loneliness* for the single adult can be faced by an active and deliberate effort to be open to many different kinds of friendships. Two or three special friends with whom single adults can share their life experiences can be an important means of helping them cope with emotional loneliness. Maintaining a close bond with family members can also be helpful. *Social loneliness* is caused partly by the reality that most of a single adult's friends are usually married. Without even realizing it, married people tend to forget to include a single friend at social events. In coping with social loneliness, the single adult can become active in a church group for single adults or find social events in the community which are as accessible to single people as they are to those who are married.

---

1. Studies show that many adolescents frequently experience loneliness. Discuss the causes of loneliness in adolescents. Also discuss some of the desirable and undesirable means that teenagers use to cope with loneliness.

2. List the pros and cons of a single adult solving a loneliness problem by living permanently with parents.

3. Some single adults are inclined to drink heavily or become workaholics in an attempt to escape from feelings of loneliness. Discuss the long-range effects in the lives of single adults who attempt to run from loneliness instead of dealing with it in a mature and positive manner.

Freedom: A Reward of the Single Life

The single adult may have more freedom than those bound by the obligations of married life. Of course, the single adult can use this freedom in a selfish way by seeking freedom from commitments to others. The playboy bachelor is a good example, or the individual who avoids marriage simply to afford living in a plush apartment and enjoying luxuries of "the good life."

Single adults are free to live a basically selfish life. But they are also free to love and serve others in ways which often are not possible for those who are married. Married people, for example, are often forced to live at great distances from ill or ageing parents because of family or work commitments. Single people, on the other hand, can be more free to live closer to their parents and to give them more care and attention in their later years.

Single people are also more free for such activities as volunteer work in a hospital, or social programs such as aid for the poor or the mentally retarded. Far from being a selfish life, the single life offers an opportunity to love and serve others. It offers the freedom to be a loving, caring person.

1. Discuss the lifestyle of the "swinging" single man or woman. In what ways is such a life essentially selfish? How would repeated sexual encounters or the search for pleasure intensify the single adult's sense of loneliness?

2. List on the board some of the other ways in which a single adult is free to love and serve others.

The Faith Dimensions of the Single Life

The single life takes on a new depth of both meaning and direction when viewed in the light of Christian faith. Christian faith provides the deeper meaning that the single life is a vocation. In other words, the church teaches that single adults have not missed their vocation by not marrying or becoming priests or religious. On the contrary, the single adult is called through baptism to live a holy Christian life, just as married people, priests, and religious are called. By trusting in God's providence and care for them, single adults can eventually come to see how their way of life is the best way to become the person God calls them to be.

Every vocation is ultimately a call to love God and others. Thus, in learning to see his or her life as a vocation, the single adult is inevitably set in the direction of learning to grow in love. Prayer is an important dimension of this growth, for prayer is essentially the giving and receiving of love between ourselves and God.

A close union with God through prayer can have a profound transforming effect on the single adult's moments alone. By prayer, the single adult can find in his or her hours of silence and solitude not simple loneliness, but union with God.

Loneliness has its source in something deeper than simply social or emotional needs. In its deepest source, loneliness arises from a person's sense of alienation from those inner values and realities which give meaning and purpose to our lives. Evidence of this is seen when a married couple is left feeling empty, if the intimacy each shares is not itself grounded in a love which transcends the passing, surface pleasures of their relationship. By the same token, a husband and wife, or two close friends whose relationship touches these inner depths, can experience a deep sense of union with one another even when they are many miles apart.

Do you sometimes feel closer to God or find it easier to pray when you are alone in your room or walking alone outdoors? What are some things that prevent us from praying when we are alone in terms of our attitude and sense of values?

If the single adult's union with God in prayer is valid, it will produce a corresponding desire to love and serve others. Sometimes this love is expressed in the quality of the single adult's love for his or her family and friends. Just as a married couple can become more loving toward one another because of their faith, so too single adults can find new depths of love for others that results from their personal union with Christ.

The single life is also particularly suited for works of Christian charity, such as participating in the Big Brother or Big Sister programs, or working as a volunteer in a home for senior citizens. The parish is important to many single people, especially when the parish acknowledges the presence of its single adult members and actively searches for their help and support.

---

1. Can you think of a single or widowed relative or friend of the family whose love has personally meant a lot to you? What does the love of this person suggest about the potential that single people have to bring happiness to the lives of others?
2. Using the board, list some other services which single people can give to their local civil or church community.

EVALUATION

Write a two- or three-page essay covering some of the main points presented here on the single life. Conclude the essay with some ideas about the single life as a vocation.

SUMMARY

1. The single life covers a broad spectrum of situations and lifestyles, among which are those of the young adult before marriage, the widowed, divorced and separated, and the adult who never marries.

2. While the single life involves an inevitable amount of loneliness, it also offers a great amount of freedom which the single adult can use for personal enrichment and the service of others.

3. The single life is a vocation. As such, it is particularly well suited for personal concern with God through prayer and Christian concern for others, by involvement in local parish and community programs.

CREATIVE ACTIVITIES

Have one or more single adults come to speak to the class as guest speakers to share their experiences as single adults.

RESEARCH PROJECTS

1. Several members of the class can look up information on Jean Vanier and Tom Dooley, both of whom were single. Report to the class about what they have done for others.

2. Others can report to the class about efforts of their parish to offer support to its single adult members, as well as what the single adults in turn can do for the parish.

Epílogue

We have examined marriage, the priesthood and religious life, and the single life. In a sense, each way of life differs greatly in what it offers and demands of those who follow it. Yet beneath these differences is a unity that is revealed by faith. Jesus made love the one common denominator of all human life. Our happiness and our fulfillment as human beings and as Christians will be measured in the end by how genuinely we loved others as Christ has loved us.

Every Christian, whether bishop or housewife, high school student or business executive, has received this call to love. The work of every Christian is at bottom the task of translating love into loving action. In the church today there is a growing awareness that *all* Christians are equally bound to this ideal of love, that is, to minister in the spirit of Christ to one another. The purpose of this concluding material is to examine the universal call to ministry that lies at the heart of each of the vocations we have discussed.

1. Listed below are a number of situations in which a group or an individual is in need of loving support from others. Gather into small groups to discuss these questions: A) what are some of the basic needs of each individual or group? B) what are some of the things that friends, family members, members of a class or members of a parish could do to help each individual or group?

A family whose house has just been destroyed by fire.

A friend or classmate whose father has died recently.

A grandparent who lives alone.

A classmate who has to stay in the hospital for two months as the result of an auto accident.

A physically or mentally handicapped child.

A racial minority family which moves into a formerly all-white neighborhood.

2. Besides the needs that arise in a particular situation, we all have inner needs; for example a need to be accepted for what we are. What are some of these less obvious but no less important needs that we all have? Who usually meets these needs for us?

Christian Mission and Ministries

In the approach to Christian ministries which we are taking here, it is important to distinguish between Christ's *mission* and his *ministries.* Jesus' mission consisted of being sent by the Father to become man, to live and die for us so that in him we might become perfectly united with the Father.

The *ministries* of Jesus are the specific means with which he carried out his mission. The National Catechetical Directory, *Sharing the Light of Faith,* published by the American bishops in 1979, suggests four fundamental ministries of Jesus; namely, the ministries of word, community building, celebration and healing service.

Every Christian shares in the one mission of Jesus. Every Christian is called by the Holy Spirit in baptism to be Christ's presence in the world today, inviting others to recognize and accept the love of the Father. Likewise, every Christian is called to share in Jesus' fourfold ministry.

In the past, the *formal* call to ministry given to members of the clergy and religious life was emphasized. This is still important today. Priests and religious provide a unique form of witness and service to the church. But today a new emphasis is placed on the *universal* call to mission which all Christians receive in baptism; emphasis is also placed on the ways in which this mission can be fulfilled by ministering to one another.

The Ministry of the Word

Jesus is the Word of God. Jesus expresses all that God is (Jn 1:1-2). Thus when he spoke of God's love he spoke out of the depths of his being. His words were God's words. They spoke the divine love for us that was expressed in the living word of Christ's whole life, and above all in his death and resurrection. His words were true in that he was what he said and said what he was: The Good News of the Father's forgiving love.

All Christians are called to share in Christ's ministry of the word. This is done in every word of love which Christians speak to one another. When husbands and wives speak words of love to one another they are ministering to each other. A ministry of the word also takes place when a high school student talks with his or her grandparents in a way that lets them know they are appreciated and loved. It is expressed in a special way whenever a word of forgiveness or acceptance is spoken in situations marked by guilt or hate. It is this kind of ministry that holds our lives together, for without it we would be left isolated and cut off from one another. This ministry of the word pertains to *all* men and women of good will, but it should be especially present among Christians. Those whose lives have been touched by God's word spoken in Christ should witness to this by the way they speak to others.

Christians must also share in Christ's ministry of the word by giving witness to Christ as Lord and Savior. In the parish community priests and deacons hold a unique place in proclaiming God's word in the Gospel and homily. But many other ministries of the word can be assumed by married and single members of the parish. Those who teach religion are ministers of God's word. Those who serve as lectors and commentators or sing in the choir are also ministers of the word.

The Ministry of Celebration

Jesus began his public ministry at a wedding celebration in Cana. He sometimes referred to his Father's kingdom as a wedding celebration, and he invites us all to the eternal celebration of the kingdom. When Jesus touched people's lives, joy often followed. It is easy to imagine the rejoicing and sense of celebration that followed the lepers' realization that they were cured or the joy of the parents whose dead daughter was raised to life. When the disciples were gathered together after Jesus' death all seemed lost. Their hopes in Jesus as the Messiah seemed shattered. But then without warning came the unexpected and unbelievable news from a jubilant Mary Magdalene, "I have seen the Lord." Suddenly those lost in despair were given a reason to celebrate.

The ministry of celebration takes place in every instance in which one person gives another a cause to rejoice: Parents who take their children on a surprise vacation; a fireman who rescues an infant from a burning building; or a high school student who helps a fellow student prepare for a difficult and important exam. Holidays, birthdays and other festive occasions also provide opportunities to celebrate—times to stop and rejoice.

All men and women need moments of celebration. All are called to help others see the good things in their lives and to celebrate them. Christians should be especially sensitive to helping others find the sometimes hidden and unnoticed reasons to celebrate. Perhaps something as simple as a beautiful sunny morning can be the occasion to join in the happiness of others who have found reason to pause, at least for a moment, to celebrate the goodness and mystery of life.

The Christian witness to Christ as the source of all celebration is expressed most perfectly in the celebration of the Eucharist. The priest plays a unique role as celebrant, but all who are present celebrate the Eucharist with the priest. In doing so they celebrate their share in Christ's victory over sin and death.

The Ministry of Community Building

Jesus lived and died so that we might enter the perfect, eternal community of love called the kingdom of God. During his earthly ministry Jesus proclaimed the Good News that, although we are sinners, we are called to the kingdom. All we have to do is repent and accept our forgiveness. Jesus' community-building ministry is portrayed in everything he said and did. His whole life can be seen as a call to enter the community of the kingdom of God.

Jesus' message is that the believer must also be a community builder. The believer must accept the one that others have rejected and forgive the one who has been a cause of pain or anxiety. He told his followers that if they have a gift to offer to God they should first go and be reconciled with the one they have wronged and then come back and offer their gift. Our unity with one another is the means through which we are to reach and experience unity with him.

The community building ministry of the risen Lord is mysteriously present every time two or more people reach out to one another. The single adult who travels a great distance in order to be with his parents for Christmas, the politician who fights for legislation assuring fair housing for minorities or better medical care for senior citizens, and high school student council representatives who plan a welcome day for incoming freshmen are all ministers of community building. Married couples express a uniquely important ministry of community building. The community of the family is the basis for all other communities.

All men and women are loved by God and are called to the community of his kingdom. Therefore, all men and women are called to the ministry of community building. But Christians should be especially sensitive to the need for community building. A Christian home, for example, should reflect Christ's community in the spirit of love and respect shown to every family member. Christians should also be sensitive to their local community, actively speaking out against any form of injustice that makes anyone or any group feel cut off from others.

Christians also need to witness to Christ as the source of all human community. This witness can be expressed in the parish (and in the Catholic school) by seeing that no one is made to feel excluded or unwanted. The pastor holds a unique place in his mission to be a focal point and stimulus to parish unity. But others can share in the leadership roles of the parish which promote parish unity. An example of this would be serving on the parish council.

The Ministry of Healing Service

Jesus healed those who suffered from physical or spiritual pain or misfortune. The lame and the blind as well as sinners found themselves healed by the sound of his voice or the touch of his hand. By dying on the cross, he revealed himself to be a God who heals us, not simply by removing our pain, but by sharing it. He served others, responded to their needs and showed them that they were not alone. God was with them and loved them in a special way.

All men and women share in this ministry of healing service by every word and every act that lessens or ends suffering in others. Doctors and others in the medical profession are obvious examples of the healing service ministry. There are many other forms of this ministry as well: the housewife who consoles a friend whose father has just died; a marriage counselor; a high school student who volunteers to work in a nursing home.

Christians should be open to ways they can participate in this ministry. Faith in Christ seems sterile if it does not bring about a deeper sense of compassion for others and a willingness to respond to their plight. Christ was quick to respond to the needs of others. So, too, Christians should be quick to notice any suffering or want in another and respond with help and healing concern.

The witness the Christian gives to Christ as the source of all healing can take many forms. On a personal basis, members of the parish can demonstrate their readiness to serve one another, perhaps in such simple gestures as making a newly divorced Catholic feel welcome or helping an elderly person up or down the stairs. Or the Christian can be active in a group which serves this ministry. Catholic organizations such as the Saint Vincent de Paul Society are vigorous in their efforts to help the poor.

Whatever our particular vocation—marriage, priesthood, religious or single life—all of us are called to share Christ's mission and ministries . . . to translate love into action.